LIVING PARABLES

LIVING PARABLES

KEVIN O'SULLIVAN, O.F.M.

FRANCISCAN HERALD PRESS
CHICAGO, ILLINOIS 60609

Living Parables by Kevin O'Sullivan O.F.M. was first published by The Bruce Publishing Company, Milwaukee, Wisconsin in 1963 and is reprinted with permission and copyright © 1979 by Franciscan Herald Press, 1434 West 51st Street, Chicago, Illinois 60609

NIHIL OBSTAT:
> ISIDORE MAHER, O.F.M.
> *Censor deputatus*

IMPRIMI POTEST:
> CELSUS O'BRIAIN, O.F.M.
> *Min. Provincial*

NIHIL OBSTAT:
> JOHN A. SCHULIEN, S.T.D.
> *Censor librorum*

IMPRIMATUR:
> ✝ ROMAN R. ATKIELSKI
> *Vicar General, Archdiocese of Milwaukee*
> *Auxiliary Bishop of Milwaukee*
> November 9, 1962

Library of Congress Cataloging in Publication Data

O'Sullivan, Kevin.
  Living Parables.
    1. Jesus Christ—Parables. I. Title
BT375.2.07   226'.8'06   79–20581
ISBN 0–8199–0780–4

MADE IN THE UNITED STATES OF AMERICA
FRANCISCAN HERALD PRESS, CHICAGO 60609

Preface

When our Lord spoke to His contemporaries in Palestine over nineteen hundred years ago, He was also speaking to you and to me. His instructions on heaven and how to get there were useful for all who wanted to go to heaven in the year three hundred and the year three thousand. With His bodily eyes He saw the groups of fishermen and farmers who listened to Him on the shore of Lake Tiberias, and the storekeepers and revenue officers who sat at His feet on the slopes of Mount Olivet, but with His divine foreknowledge He saw the millions and billions of men and women who, in all ages and in all climes, would hear His message and take it to heart. For that reason He arranged to have it preserved for us forever in the inspired Gospels which He gave to the safekeeping of His infallible Church.

It is with a part of this teaching on heaven and how to get there the following pages deal, the part namely which is preserved in what are called the gospel parables. A parable is a story describing some everyday, possible occurrence, told with the fixed purpose of conveying to the hearer some higher spiritual lesson. In other words, a parable is "an earthly story with a heavenly meaning."

The real meaning of a parable is the higher spiritual lesson the teacher intends; the earthly part is only the vehicle which conveys the spiritual message, but an understanding of the vehicle is necessary in order to grasp the point or points of the higher lesson which the teacher intends to convey.

In some thirty of these short parables our Lord has described for us the nature of the kingdom or society He is setting up on earth to bring men to heaven; the citizens who will enter it; the virtues they must develop and the vices they must avoid; the difficulties they must expect and the helps guaranteed them; and finally the infinite generosity of its King, whose rewards for His loyal subjects are beyond all human expectation. Here surely we have not only a veritable treasure-house of divine wisdom, but an inexhaustible source of encouragement and inspiration to us all in our daily uphill climb toward heaven.

For the convenience of the reader, we have grouped together into ten separate sections the parables which deal more or less with the same subject. These groups of parables do not contain all our Lord said on these subjects, but they contain enough to help us understand better the divine mysteries He graciously revealed and the obligations and privileges which are ours because of that revelation. The parables of Christ are living parables, for they are the undying word of Him who was Life itself, and they will forever be "a well springing up into life everlasting" for all those who strive to live them.

Some of these parables have appeared in *My Sunday Reading*.* With the kind permission of the publisher, we reproduce them here with some slight modifications.

* Published by The Bruce Publishing Company, Milwaukee, 1957.

Contents

ALPHABETICAL LIST OF PARABLES

LIVING PARABLES

The Nature of Christ's Kingdom

Because the Jews of His day, the Apostles and disciples included, had many erroneous ideas concerning the Messias, and the kingdom He would set up, Christ found it necessary to describe the true nature of His kingdom by means of parables. The false expectations of a Messias who would set up a universal kingdom of earthly power and glory with Israel in the seat of government were not going to be abandoned without a fight. But Christ in His divine wisdom found a means of conveying the as yet unpalatable truth in language which would be crystal clear to the well-disposed, once the realization of His true nature and mission had erased forever from their minds the false prejudices of the past.

In the following parables Christ shows that His kingdom will not be one of earthly power and splendor which comes ready-made from heaven, but must rather grow on earth from humble beginnings amid obstacles and opposition.

THE SOWER

"The same day Jesus going out of the house, sat by the sea side. And great multitudes were gathered together unto him, so that he went up into a boat and sat: and all the multitude stood on the shore. And he spoke to them many things in parables, saying: Behold the sower went forth to sow. And whilst he soweth some fell by the wayside, and the birds of the air came and ate them up. And other some fell upon stony ground, where they had not much earth: and they sprung up immediately, because they had no deepness of earth. And when the sun was up they were scorched: and because they had not root, they withered away. And others fell among thorns: and the thorns grew up and choked them. And others fell upon good ground: and they brought forth fruit, some an hundredfold, some sixtyfold, and some thirtyfold. He that hath ears to hear, let him hear" (Mt 13:1–9).

EXPLANATION: This is the first of a series of seven parables which St. Matthew has collected in the thirteenth chapter of his Gospel. Some of the seven, and perhaps all seven, were spoken by our Lord on this same occasion.

The same day: Some time during the second year of our Lord's public life. Great crowds were now following Him, and the opposition of the Pharisees was growing daily stronger and more hostile, and thus it was necessary to make known the nature of the kingdom He was about to establish.

Going out of the house: Most probably Peter's house in Capharnaum, the headquarters of His Galilean ministry.

He went up into a boat: Capharnaum is on the northwestern shore of the Sea of Galilee. Crowds had gathered around the house. He wished to preach to them, but as everyone would push and shoulder in order to get near Him, as happens in all crowds, He would neither be seen nor heard. So our Lord chose the one spot where all could see and hear Him. The shore slopes gradually toward the water and forms a natural amphitheater; sitting in the boat, which was anchored a few yards from the shore, He could be both seen and heard by all.

Behold the sower went forth to sow: The natural scene He described to the crowds was one with which they were all familiar, in fact it is possible that there was some farmer nearby at that moment doing exactly what He described. There are some stretches of good land around the Sea of Galilee, but the greater part of that district, and indeed of all Palestine, is made up of fields like the one here described by our Lord — a field, namely, that had many rocky patches, some briars and brambles, a path or paths running through it, beaten down and hardened by the constant use of the passersby, and then a few good fertile patches.

And whilst he soweth: The farmer wore an apron made of sacking, or some such material, tied around his waist. Holding the two lower corners in his left hand, he filled the apron with seed, and then, walking up one drill, he sprinkled the seed to right and left, covering about three feet on each side as he went. On the return journey, he covered another two yards, and so it went until the whole field was sown.

Fell by the wayside: Of course some of the seed fell on the pathway, which had not been plowed.

And the birds of the air came: St. Luke adds "was trodden down" (8:5). Such seed was doomed from the beginning; the passersby crushed some, and the birds devoured what was left.

Other some fell upon stony ground: Here the subsoil consisted of rock and stones. The thin layer of soil that covered the rock received the seed, and because of the heat from the rock it sprang up quickly, but just as quickly died for want of moisture; for "they had not root."

Others fell among thorns: The seed was not scattered among thornbushes already overground, but on soil underneath which the roots of thorns and brambles were already well dug in, the plow having failed to uproot them. This appears from the statement "the thorns grew up." They grew up with the growing seed, both drawing on the same soil for sustenance; but the thornbushes being more robust, the young shoots were gradually choked for want of light and nourishment and, as St. Mark adds, "yielded no fruit."

Others fell upon good ground: The sower's work was by no means all in vain. There were parts of the field free from paths, rocky subsoil, and thornbushes. In such soil the seeds took root, grew up healthy and strong, and produced a rewarding crop, yielding thirtyfold, sixtyfold, and even a hundredfold.

He that hath ears to hear, let him hear: He knew that some hearts were hardened by stubborn pride and spiritual indifference; but He had done His part — they would have only themselves to blame if they failed to grasp the truth He had offered them.

When the Apostles asked for an explanation of this parable, our Lord said: "Hear you therefore the parable of the sower. When any one heareth the word of the kingdom, and understandeth it not, there cometh the wicked one, and snatcheth away that which was sown in his heart: this is he that received the seed by the way side. And he that received the seed upon stony ground is he that heareth the word and immediately receiveth it with joy. Yet hath he not root in himself, but is only for a time: and when there ariseth tribulation and persecution because of the word, he is presently scandalized. And he that received the seed among thorns is he that heareth the word, and the care of this world and the deceitfulness of riches choketh up the word, and he becometh fruitless. But he that received the seed upon good ground, is he that heareth the word, and understandeth, and beareth fruit, and yieldeth the one an hundredfold, and another sixty, and another thirty" (Mt 13:18–23).

Hear you therefore the parable of the sower: We are fortunate indeed that the Apostles asked for an explanation of this parable. For not only have we an authentic explanation of this parable, but we have a model given us which helps to explain all His parables.

Word of the kingdom: The seed which the sower scattered is the message of salvation, brought to all men by Christ Himself, the principal sower, and by His Apostles and their successors in His kingdom the Church.

The way side: Or the path which ran through the field — the heart of one who is entirely indifferent to things spiritual, the heart namely of the skeptic, the agnostic, the materialist. He cannot avoid hearing the words.

Wicked one: The devil, however, has no difficulty in snatching away the word before it even tries to make an impression, as the birds snatched the seed from the hard, foot-trodden path.

Fell upon stony ground: This image, our Lord tells us, describes the soul of one who is superficially religious, one who is ready to be instantly interested in anything novel, but just as ready to drop it as soon as the novelty wears off and any personal effort is called for.

Yet hath he not root in himself:

Such a soul lacks the depths which make for firm convictions, and is incapable of making sacrifices for a cause which it only superficially espouses. They would gladly be Christians if it were all Mount Tabors and no Mount Calvary; they want all Easter Sundays, but no Good Fridays; crowns without crosses.

Fell among thorns: The seed that fell among the thorns fared slightly better than the two preceding classes, but only for a while. The seed had some good soil, but eventually it lost the battle, a fruitless failure.

The care of this world and the deceitfulness of riches: What the thorns and briars were to the seed, worldliness and wealth are to the Christian life: they choke and strangle it, and prevent it from bearing fruit. We have here depicted the Christian who believes the Gospel of Christ, and who appreciates its eternal values, but whose heart at the same time is centered on the pleasures of the luxuries of the body. Such a Christian would have the best of both worlds; he strives to serve two masters, but as our Lord said in another context (Mt 6:24): "No man can serve two masters. . . . You cannot serve God and mammon." However, the moderate use of worldly pleasures and wealth, within the framework of God's law, is not only permitted, but can be a great help to attaining salvation.

Fell upon good ground: The good soil receives the seed and gives it all that is necessary to produce an abundant harvest. So likewise does the well-disposed soul receive the gospel message. St. Luke (8:15) expresses this more fully when he says that the Christians represented by the good ground are those who "hearing the word, keep it, and bring forth fruit in patience." This necessary active cooperation on the part of believers is implied by St. Matthew's "understand the word," and St. Mark's "welcome the word," and by the very nature of the parable, which implies culpability on the part of the three other groups for not overcoming, or for having, their difficulties.

APPLICATION: In the audience which first heard this parable there were men and women to whom its lesson was applicable in every detail. Their minds were incapable of grasping any spiritual message. Their souls were hard as the trodden path, beaten down by years of spiritual indifference and complete neglect of all things that savored not of the world and the flesh. What their own worldly minds did not immediately crush, the devil quickly removed from their intellect "that they may not believe and be saved." This class of people were especially the Scribes and Pharisees, who had made of the religion of Moses a soul-killing, empty formula of external observances which seemed to have no purpose except to foster their own vanity and fill their wallets. Their religious power was supreme and unquestioned; all they needed now was political freedom to fill their cup of happiness. This desire for political as well as religious supremacy turned their thoughts and their hopes from the spiritual Messias-Redeemer foretold by the patriarchs and prophets to a political one who would set them free from the yoke of pagan Rome and make them a flourishing, worldly political power. When therefore they realized that

Christ's policy was not theirs, that His kingdom was not of this world, they would have none of it.

There were others among His hearers that day who were not so confirmed in their worldly outlook; in fact they had a desire for things spiritual, but it was a superficial sort of spirituality, a kind that must not interfere with their personal pleasure or cause any discomfort. Such people would gladly listen to the teaching of Christ and admire it, but they would not put it into practice.

The third group were slightly better. They accepted Christ's Gospel and realized it was the only sure way to heaven. They admitted the necessity of detachment from earthly things and the need of eternal vigilance and self-mortification, but at the same time they very· illogically thought they could indulge in the illicit joys of the senses and the sinful desires of the body, with the result that they were choked by the cares and riches and pleasures of life.

None of these three classes of people who heard the gospel message profited by it. The good seed they received brought forth no fruit; they did not win eternal life. In contrast, the Master describes the fourth group of hearers of the word, who accepted it with all its implications, and who lived up to its teaching no mattter what the cost, so that they brought forth abundant harvest, namely, of eternal happiness.

I am sure we all hope we are among the latter group. But let us look into our souls to see what kind of soil is there. Are they, perhaps, like the path in the field, open to every influence and to every strange "ism" that comes our way? Are we ever ready to question and to criticize the Church's teaching and the Church's laws? Are we of that superior intellectual type which is tolerant of every opinion except the truth? Such pride will exclude many others from the kingdom of heaven.

But the parable teaches that not only those who deliberately choose to remain outside the Church will forfeit eternal happiness, but also those who accept Christianity and then refuse to live up to its teachings. For "not every one who saith to me Lord, Lord, shall enter into the kingdom of heaven, but he that doth the will of my Father in heaven" (Mt. 7:21). The rocky subsoil of insincerity and selfishness, as well as the thorns and brambles of worldliness and sensuality, which kill the spirit of sacrifice must be removed from the soul before the gospel seed can produce its fruit. Am I striving to do just this? Am I trying to keep myself detached from the allurements of the flesh and the pleasures of the world? Am I training myself to keep that spirit of selfishness, which is in every human heart, in subjection, by gladly and willingly accepting whatever sacrifices the daily fulfillment of my duties as a Catholic entails? These are some questions we can all ask ourselves, and an honest answer will tell us if the blessed seed of the Gospel, which we fortunately have received, will die unfruitful in our souls, to our eternal loss, or will produce a great harvest of sanctity and virtue unto eternal life.

THE MUSTARD SEED

"Another parable he proposed unto them, saying: The kingdom of heaven is like to a grain of mustard seed, which a man took and sowed in his field. Which is the least indeed of all seeds; but when it is grown up, it is greater than all herbs, and becometh a tree, so that the birds of the air come, and dwell in the branches thereof" (Mt 13:31–32).

EXPLANATION: In a few simple words, easily understood by His audience, our Lord describes the kingdom He is about to found. Its beginnings will be inconspicuous, but the kingdom will be evident to the world when it reaches its full stature.

Mustard seed: Our Lord chose this simile because the contrast between the seed and the tree it produces is more noticeable than any other shrub (see Lk 17:6).

Becometh a tree: Although being only a genus of shrub, in warm climates mustard grows to a height of twelve to fifteen feet, having a stout trunk and strong branches, and so deserves to be classified as a tree.

The birds of the air: Its branches were large and strong enough to provide protection, as well as food, for flocks of birds. The little seed that produced this tree was a Jewish synonym for smallness. Thus the mustard seed was surely an apt simile for the humble beginnings of the earthly career of the Messias and of His kingdom — a carpenter's son from un-known Nazareth, born in a stable, raised in abject poverty, now living on alms and not having whereon to lay His head. His followers were a group of unlettered fishermen from Galilee, without wealth, social standing, or influence, devoid of everything deemed necessary by this world to make a success of any venture. And yet the Master foretells a magnificent future for His project: the mustard seed will spread its branches far and wide, the birds of the air — the nations of the world — will take shelter and get protection and nourishment under its shade.

Gradually our Lord taught His followers to look for the true Israel, the true kingdom of God — in the next life and not here. "Lay not up to yourselves treasures on earth," He said, "where the rust and moth consume, and where thieves break through and steal. But lay up to yourselves treasures in heaven: where neither the rust nor moth doth consume, and where thieves do not break through and steal. For where thy treasure is, there is thy heart also" (Mt 6:19–21).

APPLICATION: This parable was spoken by our Lord to instruct and to encourage His disciples in the first instance. But it has a message for His followers of every nation and of every generation: the almighty hand of God is still caring for His mustard tree — the Church; the Divine Gardener is still pruning and paring, watering and nourishing the seed which He planted on Calvary's hill, and He will continue to do so until time on earth shall end. Never in its nineteen centuries of history has the mustard tree spread its branches so widely as in our own day, and never in its centuries of growth has it experienced such violent, organized opposition as it is experiencing today. Both facts are convincing proofs of God's abiding presence in His Church: "Behold I am with you all days, even to the consummation of the world" (Mt 28:20), and "If the world hate you, know ye that it hath hated me before you. If you had been of the world, the world would love its own: but because you are not of the world, but I have chosen you out of the world, therefore the world hateth you" (Jn 15:18–19).

How grateful should we Catholics be that we are privileged to be resting under this divinely planted tree. How gladly should we shoulder every burden that Christ places upon us in order to help its growth. Millions of our brothers — fellow children of God — are still far from its protection and shade; and there are other thousands who are wasting their time and their God-given strength striving to destroy the divinely protected mustard tree. We have a grave, a serious, obligation to help these brothers save their souls. Blinded as they are by ignorance and sinful pride, they cannot find their way unaided to this tree of life. Christ, our Savior and theirs, expects us and asks us to stretch out a helping hand to them, to lead them to safety. Would we refuse Him this little return for all that He has done for us? He does not ask us all to leave our homes and our families in order to spread His kingdom. He has so kindly and so divinely arranged things that the vast majority of Catholics can and should be apostles while still caring for a family and following their ordinary earthly vocation.

The first apostolic activity each one can and must carry out is the sanctification of self by daily living the Christian life. This may not appear at first sight to be of help to others but it is, for the greater the fervor of each individual the greater will be the fervor of the whole Church, the more abundant will the divine grace be and the greater will the Church's attraction be for those outside.

Second, active cooperation, under the direction of our spiritual leaders, is the duty of each of us if we are for Christ. This cooperation can take many forms, such as contributing according to our means to the financial needs of missionary enterprises; helping the spread of Catholic literature; getting, through study circles and private reading, a deeper knowledge of the faith in order to be able to stand up fearlessly for Christian truths and Christian virtue in our home, in our factory or office, and in our places of leisure and recreation; giving of our time to spiritual and corporal works of mercy.

The sincere, active, burning love for God and neighbor which motivated the early Christians brought the Roman empire to the feet of Christ. The same true, living, ardent charity will win over our contemporaries if we but do our part. Christianity has not failed, but far too many Christians have failed Christianity. The Gospel is still "the power of God unto salvation" (Rom 1:16), if only those who possess it will "let their light shine before men." Have I been doing so up until now? Have I been an inspiration and a guide to my neighbor? If not, there is still time. Saul was for years an avowed opponent of Christ. He saw the light on the road to Damascus, and became St. Paul, the great Apostle of the Gentiles.

THE LEAVEN IN THE FLOUR

"Another parable he spoke to them: The kingdom of heaven is like to leaven, which a woman took and hid in three measures of meal, until the whole was leavened" (Mt. 13:33).

EXPLANATION: In the preceding parable, our Lord describes the external, visible growth of the kingdom. In the present parable He describes the mysterious interior, secret power of His kingdom, which produces a complete transformation of all that comes under its influence.

The simile He used to describe this power was well known to His hearers. Bread was the staple food of the people, and it was the task of the woman of the house to bake the necessary bread. To do this, she first wet a quantity of flour with water or milk, and adding a small amount of leaven, she kneeded the mixture until it became a consistent dough. It was then ready for baking. Bread made without leaven was sometimes eaten, but only as an emergency ration, for it was insipid and unpalatable. The Jews were commanded by the Mosaic law to eat unleavened bread during the Passover festival to remind them of the hardships and slavery they endured in Egypt, but for the other fifty-one weeks of the year leavened bread was the daily diet of the people.

The penetrating, invigorating power of the minute bit of leaven which made it capable of fermenting a large mass of flour, and of converting it from an inert and tasteless mass into a nourishing and pleasing food, was common knowledge. Therefore, when the Master says now that His kingdom is like leaven, they understand the simile.

The three measures of flour mentioned were the ordinary quantity used by a housewife who baked a few times a week for a large family. The quantity of leaven is very small in relation to the quantity of flour, but the secret, imperceptible power of transformation possessed by the leaven is the point of the discussion. The woman who "hid" the leaven in the flour and proceeded to kneed the dough need be of no special significance. As the piece of leaven stirs up, energizes, and transforms the mass of flour, so will Christ's Gospel and the power of His kingdom give a new life and new energy to those who will receive it. This is the essential, central lesson of this parable.

A glance at the pages of early Christian history will show us how this parable was fulfilled to the letter. The kingdom of God — the Church — with its life-bearing channels of supernatural grace, the seven sacraments, was placed in the very center of the then-known world. It was placed there without the world knowing it, as the woman "hid" the leaven in the flour, for the contemporaries of Christ were ignorant of His presence among them. What John the

Baptist said to the Pharisees: "But there hath stood one in the midst of you, whom you know not" (Jn 1:26), could be applied to the civil leaders of the people also: "He came unto His own, and His own received Him not." The same was true of His Church, it was in the midst of the world and the world knew it not; but like the hidden leaven it was simmering and fermenting quietly, imperceptibly permeating and changing the mass of humanity in whose midst it had been hidden.

APPLICATION: Looking down from the vantage point which nineteen centuries of Church history give us, we can clearly see the transformation brought about in the world by the kingdom of God, the Church. This transformation was brought about not by force of arms, nor strength of armies, not by dialectical skill nor by human eloquence; it was brought about from within by the silent flame of divine grace which quietly and almost imperceptibly set the hearts of individuals afire with love of God. Pagan Rome became Christian Rome; the seat of worldly dominion became the center of the spiritual kingdom of God. Gradually the leaven of divine grace spread beyond the bounds of the empire. Today, however, while there are still some who have not accepted Christ's Gospel, there are none who have not benefited by the blessings He brought on earth.

Our first reaction to this must be to say a heartfelt "thank you" to the Father of mercies, who has been so kind and so generous to this unworthy world of ours. Nothing short of the divine power of Christ can explain the growth and the spread of His Church in the face of obstacles, human and superhuman, which would have overwhelmed any man-made institution.

A second reaction should be a brief look into our own consciences. We have not only benefited by the divine leaven, we have become leaven and must act as such. Just as every bit of dough which has been leavened is capable of leavening other dough, so the Christian who has been blessed with the gift of faith and God's grace is capable, and has the obligation, of spreading these gifts among his fellow men. But in order to leaven, to Christianize, others, he must be truly leavened, truly Christian, himself. His Christianity must not be an external cloak which he wears for an hour on Sunday morning, and locks in his wardrobe for the rest of the week. No, it must be part and parcel of his very life; in it he must "live, move, and have his being." The fire of divine love which burns within the Christian who so lives his faith will spread its light and its warmth among those he meets. Almost unknown to himself he will be the leaven of his neighbors.

Am I such a Christian? Do I appreciate the great gift of faith God has given me, and do I lead others to appreciate it? Will it be said of me when I die that the world was a better place because I lived in it? You can give the answer now. Begin today (if you are not already doing so) to be a true leaven in the midst of your fellow men, a true helper to your neighbor on the road to heaven. Remember, you will pass through this world only once.

THE HIDDEN TREASURE
AND THE PRECIOUS PEARL

"The kingdom of heaven is like unto a treasure hidden in a field. Which a man having found, hid it, and for joy thereof goeth, and selleth all that he hath, and buyeth that field. Again the kingdom of heaven is like a merchant seeking good pearls. Who when he had found one pearl of great price, went his way and sold all that he had, and bought it" (Mt 13:44–46).

EXPLANATION: In the preceding parables, our Lord describes His kingdom in relation to all peoples — it is a tree which will continue to grow and expand until it gives food and shelter to all nations; it is leaven which will transform and give new life to the world. In the passage above He describes His kingdom as the greatest of all treasures that each individual can acquire. The two images He uses, the "treasure hidden" and the "pearl of great price," were readily understood by His listeners. In a country like Palestine, so frequently overrun by invaders, it was customary for people to bury their gold and other precious possessions in tombs or in caves or in the fields when they heard an invader was approaching. It often happened that the owner was killed or disappeared, and all knowledge of the hidden treasure disappeared with him (the scrolls recently discovered in the caves of Qumran near the Dead Sea were hidden there over nineteen centuries ago). The possibility therefore of unearthing a treasure chest in any part of Palestine or in other countries of the Middle East was not as remote as it would be in Western countries.

The hidden treasure is described by our Lord as having been found accidentally by one who was working in another man's field. The workman immediately reburies the treasure lest anybody else should find it, and then sells everything he has so he is able to buy the field from the farmer, thus making himself undisputed owner of the treasure. That the hidden treasure was not buried by the owner of the field is evident, or he would not have sold his field. By becoming owner of the field the workman became legal owner of the hidden treasure according to the Jewish and Roman law, but he seemed to deceive the farmer by keeping silent about the hidden treasure. He could have removed the treasure secretly if he were not concerned with justice; therefore it would appear he felt he was acting justly by fulfilling the letter of the law. However that may be, it must be borne in mind that not every point in the material side of a parable is held up for praise and imitation by the Master, but only those points which convey the spiritual lesson he wishes to inculcate.

In these two parables the lesson is the same: the incomparable worth of the kingdom of heaven and the wise man giving all he has in order to "purchase" it. But there is this difference between the two parables: the workman in the field finds the treasure accidentally, he was not looking for any such treasure; whereas the merchant was searching for the precious pearl. Did our Lord have in mind the Gentiles, to whom the kingdom of God came unexpectedly, and the pious Jews, who were looking forward and searching anxiously for the kingdom? Possibly so, but this does not exclude the many others who down through the ages would discover the kingdom of God, the Church of Christ, casually and accidentally as it were — St. Paul, St. Augustine, and St. Ignatius Loyola come to mind — and the many who searched diligently until they found the precious pearl, such as the first Apostles, St. Francis, St. Dominic, and a host of others down to our own day.

APPLICATION: There is a lesson for all of us in these two parables: we are called on to imitate these two wise men in order that we might possess the eternal happiness of God's heavenly kingdom. The first step toward this end is to become members of God's visible kingdom on earth, the Church. There and there only can be found the ways and means which can lead to the possession of the treasure. Christ has deposited in His Church not only the maps and charts which show the right road to the treasure, but the transport and aids which will get us there. There are many sincere men, no doubt, who for one reason or another cannot see the necessity of taking this first step. If their reasons are sincere, God will find other means of leading them to their destination. But far greater is the number who are held back by self-love.

This same self-love will also prevent many of those who have taken the first step from securing the eternal treasure. As members of Christ's kingdom on earth we must never forget that we have still to give our all if we are to purchase the great treasure of eternal happiness. These are the words of Christ Himself: "Not every one that saith to me, Lord, Lord, shall enter into the kingdom of heaven: but he that doth the will of my Father who is in heaven, he shall enter into the kingdom of heaven" (Mt 7:21). It is not enough, therefore, that we be baptized Catholics, and that we recognize Christ as our leader and our Lord; we must carry out faithfully the commandments of God and of the Church. We must, in other words, "take up our cross daily." This is where self-love steps in. This is where the earthly body, which is part of our human makeup, cries out in rebellion and refuses the cross. The wise men in the parables gave everything in order to possess the treasure. Most of us are willing to give something, many are willing to give a lot, but very few today are willing to give their all in exchange for the pearl of great price.

Does this "giving all" mean that we are all expected to abandon the world and take on the religious vows of poverty, chastity, and obedience? There are many who do just this, but this is not the only way, in fact it is not the normal way Christ expects us to purchase the eternal treasure. Heaven is within the reach of all men and women who, while following the ordinary vocations of life and partaking of this world's joys and pleasures within the framework of God's commandments, never lose sight of the goal toward which they are moving. But keeping within the framework of the commandments is the difficulty. We do not have a vow of obedience, but we must be obedient to all lawful authority placed over us. We may possess the goods of this world, but only such goods as we lawfully and justly acquire; nor may we withhold all of these from a fellow man in need. We need not take a vow of chastity, but yet we must be chaste; we must use the gifts and the pleasures of sex only within the limits set down by God's wise laws. Yes, living our daily lives within the framework of God's laws is not at all easy for our human nature, but it was never intended to be easy. Giving one's all is a sacrifice, it always was and it always will be. The merchant and the finder in the parables made a big sacrifice when they gave up everything they possessed, but in comparison with what they received in return, this sacrifice looked trivial to them. We, too, in our sane and serious moments, do not doubt that eternal happiness is worth more than all the kingdoms of this world, and yet how many there are who sell this birthright for a "mess of pottage," a momentary illicit pleasure, a crafty dishonest gain, a passing gratification of personal pride.

Our twentieth century, it is true, is so engrossed in providing for the earthly comforts and pleasures of the body, and so devoid of any spiritual outlook, that even those who firmly know and believe that there is an eternity to follow after death find it hard to allow their faith and convictions to govern their daily actions. Yet the evil example of others will never justify man's wrongdoing. The commandments of God are still binding, even though they are openly and flagrantly violated by individuals and by nations today. We will not be asked at the judgment: "What did your neighbors do?" but "What did you do?" If we lose the pearl of great price — the eternity of happiness God has offered us — it will not be the fault of others. The fault will be ours and ours only. We refused to pay the price. We did not think it worth the paltry "all" which we had in this life.

THE SEED GROWING SECRETLY

"And he said: So is the kingdom of God, as if a man should cast seed into the earth, and should sleep and rise, night and day, and the seed should spring, and grow up whilst he knoweth not. For the earth of itself bringeth forth fruit, first the blade, then the ear, afterwards the full corn in the ear. And when the fruit is brought forth, immediately he putteth in the sickle, because the harvest is come" (Mk 4:26–29).

EXPLANATION: This parable, reported in St. Mark only, also deals with the kingdom of heaven, the kingdom Christ was setting up on earth, and it was spoken by our Lord in order to remove a misunderstanding which was very much in the Apostles' minds. Because of the imagery used by the authentic prophets and the exaggerations developed in the noninspired literature of the Jews, the Apostles and their contemporaries had many erroneous ideas concerning the Messias and His kingdom. One such idea was that the Messias would come on earth in a blaze of glory, backed by astounding divine miracles and portents, subduing all opposition and establishing a universal kingdom of earthly peace and prosperity under the dominion of Israel. The Apostles expected Christ to quickly fulfill these expectations, and so He had to wean them gradually from these false views (James and John, for example, expected Him to call down fire from heaven on the Samaritan village which refused to receive Him [cf. Lk 9:54]). This parable was one of the means He used to bring home to them that the founding of His kingdom would be brought about quietly, patiently, and almost imperceptibly, without startling heavenly signs or earthly cataclysms.

The kingdom of God, as if a man should cast seed into the earth: Just as a farmer, having plowed his field, casts the seed into the soil, covers it up, and leaves the rest to nature.

And should sleep and rise, night and day: Having done his part of the planting, the farmer now goes about his other duties. He does not sit in his plowed field waiting for the seed to sprout, nor does he do anything to hasten its sprouting. He knows this is unnecessary, for he has planted healthy seed in receptive soil.

The seed should spring . . . up whilst he knoweth not: It would seem the farmer had forgotten the seed he planted; he is busy over other duties when it springs up.

The earth of itself . . . : But the farmer had done all that was necessary; the natural laws of the Creator did the rest. The silent miracle of nature turned the lone seed into, first, a tiny green blade, then the blade became a sturdy stalk, the stalk in turn produced the ear or grain pod, and finally the ear filled with many seeds similar to the one that entered the earth.

Immediately he putteth in the sickle: Then the farmer becomes active once more. The harvest time has arrived in due season. The grain is ready, and he reaps it and puts it in his barn.

APPLICATION: Christ used this simple, everyday example to show His Apostles and followers that the growth of His kingdom, His Church on earth, would be gradual, almost imperceptible, while men went about their ordinary occupations, but behind it is the power of God who uses the secondary causes He Himself has created to produce not only material but also spiritual results. Christ the Son of God compared Himself to the farmer: He had tilled the ground and prepared the soil; He was now planting the seed, the gospel message; and He assured His followers that an abundant harvest would follow in due course. Apart from the Jewish nationalistic idea of a temporal messianic kingdom of which they gradually rid themselves, there was the evident obstacle of the pharisaic opposition to His Teaching, an opposition which was preventing the seed of the spiritual kingdom from taking root. Why would He not remove this opposition, they thought, by using the divine powers He possessed? But He would not. It was little wonder then that the Apostles thought that Christ had failed, and His enemies had conquered, when He was condemned to death. Yet this was but the silent mysterious growth of the seed. The arrest of Christ in Gethsemani unlocked the fetters that bound the human race; His death on the cross was the source of eternal life for mankind. The seed, cast in the ground and apparently forgotten, sprang forth at the right moment, and produced abundant fruit. This the Apostles understood in its full light after the descent of the Holy Ghost on Pentecost. For they too (the weaklings who had fled on Holy Thursday night) went forth bravely and gladly to offer their earthly lives for the spread of Christ's kingdom so that their fellow men could gain eternal life.

While no Christian today will question the infinite wisdom of God's providence in founding and establishing His Church on earth, many Christians fail to see the same omnipotent providence building the kingdom of God in their individual souls. While admitting that Christ "had to suffer and die" in order to redeem them, they forget His command to take up their own cross daily if they wish to follow Him into eternal glory. Such souls quickly grow impatient when they find the road to heaven seemingly blocked by man-made obstacles or human weaknesses — of self or others. Does God care any more, they cry, or is He leaving us to our fate? He planted the seed; He gave them the faith and their particular vocation, but now He has evidently gone about His business and forgotten them. If the seed in the parable could reason, it too would most likely have felt that it had been abandoned — the farmer had left it and was now busy with other cares — yet that very abandonment was necessary. He knew the powers given to nature by the Creator, and he was confident of success. The results proved his wisdom. So it is also with God's dealings with souls. When it seems to them that God has abandoned them, His omnipotent grace is working secretly, underground, helping them to overcome the obstacles and to bear the weight of trouble and sorrow which seems about to smother them. Like the seed, in due course they will emerge from the gloom and darkness of the undersoil to enjoy God's warming sunlight and to produce fruit for eternity.

But in the meantime, during the hours of darkness which may seem so long to most of us, we must retain an unshakable confidence in God's infinite wisdom and love. We cannot see the whys and the wherefores of the many hard knocks which life inflicts on us, but we can be certain that there is a reason for each one, for each is part of the divine pattern which our loving Father has planned for our eternal destiny. If, aided by His grace, we "wait patiently on the Lord," doing our part and confidently trusting in Him to do His, we need have no anxiety about the outcome. Like the Master we have been called to follow, we will pass successfully through our Gethsemanis and Calvaries to rise triumphantly from Olivet's hill, but on this condition only, that while stretching out our eager hands for the eternal crown we do not try to sidestep the cross which alone will lead us to it.

Why the Mixture of Good and Evil?

Because of their age-old national prejudices, it took the Jews some time to grasp the fact that Christ came on earth to set up a spiritual, not a political, kingdom. After they finally grasped this truth, they expected then that His spiritual kingdom would be a gathering, a congregation, of saintly men and women who would detach themselves from sin and from the world and give themselves entirely to God. This was a very natural and human conclusion. If Christ, the Son of God, came on earth to bring men to heaven, surely they should go willingly and directly there. But Christ knew human nature. He, in His divine knowledge, foresaw that many would refuse to accept the offer of salvation, and that of those who accepted it, not all would be willing to keep themselves free at all times from earthly entanglements and sin. The devil, the archenemy of God and of man, would still be permitted to exercise his evil art of seduction and temptation on earth. In this he is, unwittingly, actually cooperating with God, for it is God's plan that men should be tempted and tried in the earthly kingdom, so as to prove themselves worthy of the everlasting kingdom in heaven.

The Church, therefore, will always be troubled and tormented by enemies within and without its fold. Our Lord has foretold us this, so that we would forearm ourselves. To the enemies we must not react with impatience or vengefulness. We must imitate the patience and charity of our Master. St. Mary Magdalene, St. Mary of Egypt, St. Augustine, St. Ignatius, St. Francis, and a million other unknown saints did just that. And they are saints in heaven because they followed Christ's example.

THE WHEAT AND THE WEEDS

"Another parable he proposed to them, saying: The kingdom of heaven is likened to a man that sowed good seed in his field. But while men were asleep, his enemy came and oversowed cockle among the wheat, and went his way. And when the blade was sprung up, and had brought forth fruit, then appeared also the cockle. And the servants of the goodman of the house coming said to him: Sir, didst thou not sow good seed in thy field? whence then hath it cockle? And he said to him: An enemy hath done this. And the servants said to him: Wilt thou that we go and gather it up? And he said: No, lest perhaps, gathering up the cockle, you root up the wheat also together with it. Suffer both to grow until the harvest, and in the time of the harvest I will say to the reapers: Gather up first the cockle, and bind it into bundles to burn, but the wheat gather ye into my barn" (Mt 13:24-30).

EXPLANATION:

The kingdom of heaven: The Son of God took on human nature in order to earn heaven for all mankind. His coming was first announced in the Garden of Eden after Adam's sin (cf. Gn 3:15), and was repeated again and again through the patriarchs and the prophets. He was to be king, prophet, and priest, and as each of these was inducted into his office by anointing with oil, the promised Redeemer gradually came to be known as the Anointed, the *Messias* in Hebrew, *Christos* in Greek. His kingdom was to be universal, its subjects coming from the four corners of the earth (cf. Mt 8:11; 24:14), not restricted to Palestine as the Pharisees wrongly imagined. His purpose in this parable, and in the following parables, is to explain the nature of His kingdom. It has two stages: the one here on earth, a visible society founded by Christ to prepare all those who will enter it and will accept its teaching and helps; and the second stage, the perfect society in the afterlife, in heaven, where all its citizens who prepared and proved themselves in the first stage will have everlasting happiness in the company of God. It is of the first stage that our Lord speaks here, and in most of the following parables, for He is intent on showing what men must do and what they must expect if they will follow Him and make themselves worthy of the second stage.

Sowed good seed: Again the simile is taken from agricultural life. The seed itself has no admixture of weeds.

Men were asleep: Under cover of darkness, at night namely.

His enemy came and oversowed cockle among the wheat: A cunning but wicked way to prevent the sower from having an abundant crop in his field.

When the blade . . . brought forth fruit: It was only then the weeds were noticed, a fact which leads all interpreters to conclude that the weed was the *darnel*, the blade of which is not distinguishable from the wheat stalk. Only when both put forth their fruit can one distinguish them.

An enemy hath done this: The sower knew that his field was good and also that his wheat seed was perfect. There was but one explanation then for the appearance of the weeds: it was the work of a bitter enemy. Such a method of injuring a neighbor was not unknown in the East at the time of our Lord, and even in later days, and so the farmer is not surprised.

Lest perhaps, gathering up the cockle: The servants were most anxious to have a good wheat crop. The wheat stalks would grow stronger and their yield would be greater if they had the full nourishment of the soil to themselves, but the farmer knew that some wheat stalks would be destroyed if the darnel were removed now.

The harvest: Then the separation can be safely made; the weeds will be food for fire but the wheat will be safely stored in the barn.

At the request of the disciples, our Lord explained this parable thus: "He that soweth the good seed, is the Son of man. And the field, is the world. And the good seed are the children of the kingdom. And the cockle, are the children of the wicked one. And the enemy that sowed them, is the devil. But the harvest is the end of the world. And the reapers are the angels. Even as cockle therefore is gathered up and burned with fire: so shall it be at the end of the world. The Son of man shall send his angels, and they shall gather out of his kingdom all scandals, and them that work iniquity. And shall cast them into the furnace of fire: there shall be weeping and gnashing of teeth. Then shall the just shine as the sun, in the kingdom of their Father. He that hath ears to hear, let him hear" (Mt 13:37–43).

Son of man: One of many titles applied to the Messias in the Old Testament, and the one which Christ most frequently applies to Himself. In the Gospel of St. Matthew, He calls Himself the Son of man twenty-nine times, while neither the disciples nor the people ever call Him by that name. It would seem that Christ chose this title for Himself in order to stress the reality and the humility of His incarnation. He who is God is become one of us, "one tempted in all things like as we are, without sin" (Heb 4:15).

The field, is the world: The Son of man, the promised Redeemer, came to save the whole world. He was the Messias not only of the Jews, but of all people, for all time, until the final harvest.

Children of the kingdom: Those who would accept and profit by His message and means of salvation will be heirs of His kingdom, His brothers, and adopted sons of God the Father.

Children of the wicked one: The weeds sown among the wheat are those who allow themselves to become the adopted children of Satan.

The enemy . . . is the devil: The devil is the leader of the angels who, because of pride, rebelled against God and were cast out forever from heaven. They were spiritual beings, and they still retain their angelic nature, but the exercise of their power is subject to God's permission. From the beginning the devil was the sworn enemy of the human race. In the Garden of Eden, through lies and falsehoods he induced Adam and Eve to sin: "You shall be as Gods" (Gn 3:1–6). Down through the ages, he led men away from their Creator, and got them to adore false gods. As soon as the work of redemption began, he and his assistants put forth all their efforts to thwart this work, lest mankind should be brought back to God. The temptation of our Lord after the forty days' fast, which of course failed miserably (cf. Mt 4:3–11), was the signal for this all-out effort, and it continued until Satan and his followers (cf. Jn 8:42–44) had nailed Christ to the cross on Calvary, not realizing that that very cross was the key that reopened heaven. Though he failed to prevent the reopening of heaven and the establishment of God's kingdom on earth, Satan continued, and will continue, to use every endeavor within the limits set for him by God, to prevent man from reaching heaven. Our parable describes this ceaseless evildoing of Satan. He cannot prevent the growth and progress of the kingdom of God, but he can make its growth and its propagation very difficult. For this he uses his earthly agents, "his children," whom he plants among the faithful in secret "while men were asleep." Under the cloak of zeal for God's house and His kingdom, these "children of Satan" spread their heresies and their schisms, their liberalisms and their modernisms, among the "children of the kingdom," and their greatest menace lies in the fact that, because of their clever camouflage, they are well established before they are recognized as enemies (cf. 2 Cor 11:14).

The harvest is the end of the world: It is God's will that Satan and his agents should be permitted, within well-defined limits, to tempt and prove the fidelity of the just. However, on the day of final judgment the children of God will all be placed in the kingdom of eternal peace and happiness, while Satan and his followers will enter into their abode of eternal suffering and despair.

The reapers are the angels: The good angels shall accompany our Lord when He comes for the general judgment on the last day (cf. Mt 24:31), and shall separate the wicked from the just (cf. Mt 13:49).

Cast them into the furnace of fire: The lot of the children of Satan will be like that of the weeds, they shall be condemned to a furnace of fire, but unlike the weeds their sufferings will be everlasting, as is clear from our Lord's own description of the last judgment: "Depart from me, you cursed, into *everlasting* fire, prepared for the devil and his angels" (Mt 25:41; cf. Lk 16:24).

Weeping and gnashing of teeth: This same phrase is used in Mt 22:13 to describe the reaction of the wicked on receiving their condemnatory sentence. The weeping is a consequence of the eternal loss they will have to endure, and the gnashing of teeth is caused by the positive pain which they now fully perceive to be theirs forever. This is the constant teaching of the Church, and one fact alone is sufficient proof of this truth: Christ, the Son of God, became man and endured all the agonies of His crucifixion in order to save us from such a fate.

Then shall the just shine as the sun: The full glory of the just will begin only at the general judgment. The souls of the just will be reunited to their risen bodies, glorified now and free from all defects of age or infirmity. The light of glory, the Beatific Vision which the soul will then enjoy, will illumine the risen body also, and make it "shine as the sun," as our Lord's body shone on Mount Tabor during the transfiguration (cf. Mt 17:2).

Kingdom of their Father: The perfect kingdom of God in heaven, the continuation and perfection of the kingdom Christ set up on earth, will be shared by all the just with God their Father.

For by becoming followers of Christ, and His brothers as well, through the sacrament of Baptism, men become children of God and heirs of His kingdom.

He that hath ears to hear: Once more our Lord warns the disciples, as He warned the multitudes in the preceding parable, to heed His words and to learn the lesson He had just taught them.

APPLICATION: There was a very necessary lesson in this parable for the disciples and the first followers of Christ. They had the erroneous idea that the kingdom Christ was setting up on earth would be composed of the "pure, holy, and undefiled" only, and furthermore that Christ, who claimed to be God and whom they were coming to believe was God, would exterminate Satan and all his followers from the face of the earth. But the Master tells them in this parable that His plan is not theirs; He will bear with the weeds — the children of Satan — and give them every opportunity of turning to Him until they irrevocably exclude themselves from His company. And because Satan will continue to be God's enemy until the end, and will have followers in every generation, the children of God on earth must expect opposition and trials. The Apostles did not grasp the full meaning of this teaching until they received the Holy Ghost on Pentecost. But from that day on, they cheerfully and eagerly accepted the doctrine of the cross and they preached it to their people.

This is the lesson we too must learn from this parable. The words of our Lord: "He that has ears to hear let him hear," were addressed to us too. It is by God's permission and for our good that Satan and his followers are permitted to work among us. God is using them as a means to enable us to prove ourselves worthy of His kingdom. But because of the weakness of human nature we, all of us, find it hard to accept this necessity of suffering as a part of our formation. We would all prefer it if the road to heaven could be a path of roses without any thorns. This, however, is not God's plan. We have it on the word of our Lord Himself: "If any man will come after me, let him deny himself, and take up his cross and follow me" (Mt 16:24); and again, "He that taketh not up his cross, and followeth me, is not worthy of me" (Mt 10:38). This is also the teaching of this parable: we must bear with evil; we must expect temptations and trials, and by triumphing over them, prove ourselves worthy of Him. With nineteen centuries of Church history to instruct and convince us, it ought to be much easier for us to grasp this truth and apply it to ourselves. The Roman persecutions spread the faith around the empire; the blood of martyrs was indeed the seed of Christianity. The early heresies were the crucible in which the gold of the true doctrine was separated from the dross. And in almost every century Satan has planted noxious weeds among the good wheat, with the express purpose of preventing its growth. To Satan's chagrin, the wheat has grown stronger and increased its yield. But this is so only because individual members of the Church, relying on God's grace and infallible promise, took up their crosses cheerfully.

You and I have our part to play in the field of the Lord, the Church. We are little blades of wheat surrounded on all sides by weeds, whose aim is to prevent us from bringing forth good fruit. Our greatest danger lies in this, that the weeds can camouflage themselves as friends. When the going is hard, when the keeping of God's commandments is anything but easy for weak human nature, when our shoulders are feeling the bruises caused by the daily crosses, then the enemy will whisper: "Take it easy. Do you have to do all that? Surely God never meant you to put up with so-and-so. Use your intelligence; take the easy way out; enjoy life while you can. There is lots of time to worry about your soul. A loving Father like God wouldn't want you to suffer in this manner. Your body was given you to use and enjoy; that talk of bearing your cross is outdated, who believes in it any more?" These are the whisperings of an enemy pretending to be a friend, the age-old strategem used by Satan on Eve: Eat of the fruit, you shall not die; rather, by disobeying, you shall be as gods, completely free from all restrictions (cf. Gn 3:1–5). The surprising thing is that any of us could be taken in by such a camouflage. And yet, how often have we left the solid highway of mortification to wallow in the mire of earthly gratification and bodily pleasure, all because of a suggestion from our oldest enemy posing as our best friend.

Let us never forget it, Satan is still active in the world. He will always find the most suitable fifth columnist to place in our midst. His offer is ever the same: "All the kingdoms of the world, and all the earthly joys thereof will I give thee, if only you will desert from the kingdom of God"; but he does color his offer with the tint that is most attractive to each individual. He never asks us to sin; that would be crude. Instead, he finds a convenient justification for every violation of every commandment and of every law. He pretends his concern is for our health, our personal liberty, our status in society, our future security, our present happiness, our earthly welfare, when all the time his one ambition is to draw us away from allegiance to God's kingdom.

This parable of the weeds was a forewarning, to the Apostles and to us: that we shall not be members of the Church triumphant unless we have proved ourselves worthy soldiers of the Church Militant. The heavenly crown of glory is reserved for those who have willingly worn the earthly crown of thorns.

THE SEINE NET

"Again the kingdom of heaven is like a net cast into the sea, and gathering together of all kinds of fishes. Which, when it was filled, they drew out, and sitting by the shore, they chose out the good into vessels, but the bad they cast forth. So shall it be at the end of the world. The angels shall go out, and shall separate the wicked from among the just. And shall cast them into the furnace of fire: there shall be weeping and gnashing of teeth" (Mt 13:47–50).

EXPLANATION: This parable also is concerned with the coexistence of bad and good people in the kingdom of God on this earth. While the stress in the parable of the wheat and the weeds is on the necessity of patience on the part of the good, the emphasis here is on the fate that awaits the wicked. The wicked may appear to be equal to the good in this world, they may even boast of being happier and more fortunate, but the day of reckoning for them will come.

A net cast into the sea: The image our Lord uses to convey His lesson was one easily understood by His audience. Fishing was the means of livelihood of many who dwelt around the shores of the Sea of Galilee. The net mentioned was a seine net, still used today in many parts of the world. It varied in length from one hundred to several hundred yards, and its depth depended on the depth of the sea or lake bed in which it was used. It was weighted on one side with lead or stones, while a row of corks or light pieces of wood kept the upper end floating on top of the water. While one boat and crew held on to the floating end of the net, the other boat, in which the net was loaded, made a large sweep of the lake or sea dropping the net as it went, and returned to the first boat to join both ends of the net. Then the net

and its contents were dragged to the shore.

All kinds of fishes: As the net enclosed everything in its path, there were fishes included that were not fit to eat, and therefore of no use to the fishermen. Unsuitable fish would be gathered from any lake or sea, but it was especially so in Palestine where the Mosaic law had declared certain classes of fish unclean, i.e., not fit for human consumption.

But the bad they cast forth: When the net had been hauled ashore, the fisherman sat down and sorted their catch. The good fish were put into receptacles to be taken home or to the market, but the bad were cast on the shore to rot or become food for the birds.

So shall it be at the end of the world: The scene He has described was familiar to everybody, and our Lord now gives it its higher spiritual meaning. The seine net represents the kingdom He is founding on earth, His Church. The sea over which it is spread is this world. The fishes stand for the men and women who were gathered into the Church, and the fishermen are Christ Himself and His helpers, the Apostles and their successors, who offer the means of salvation, the Gospel, to all. But of the many who will come into the net, that is, accept the Gospel, there will be a number who will fail to pass the test of worthiness when the final sorting day comes.

The angels shall go out, and shall separate the wicked from among the just: What the fishermen do with their catch the angels will do for all mankind at the general judgment — they will separate the wicked from the just (cf. previous parable — Mt 13:41). In His own description of the last judgment, our Lord says that He, accompanied by the angels, shall separate the two groups (cf. Mt 25:32).

And shall cast them into the furnace of fire: The punishment of the wicked will be twofold: separation from the just, that is, the Beatific Vision of God for all eternity, and some material or quasi-material form of punishment which our Lord describes as the "furnace of fire." The first punishment, commonly called the pain of loss, will be the greater of the two. This is the essence of damnation, as the term itself indicates, derived from the Latin word *damnum* meaning "loss." Added to this eternal loss is the pain of sense, a suffering inflicted on the souls, and after the general resurrection, on the bodies also of the damned. This pain of sense is caused by fire, we are told in Scripture, but we are not told the exact nature of that fire. That it is not a material fire, as our earthly fires are, is clear from the fact that it was prepared for the devil and his bad angels, who are spirits and cannot be affected by material objects. "Furnace of fire," therefore, is not a metaphor to describe the spiritual and mental sufferings of the damned caused by their sense of loss, but is some additional reality, objectively present outside the sufferer, and the external cause of other torments over and above the pain of loss.

There shall be weeping and gnashing of teeth: This image describes the reaction of the damned to the two torments spoken of above. The gnashing or grinding of teeth is a natural reaction to physical pain. The damned will be constrained to gnash and grind their teeth for all eternity, for the pain of sense they suffer will be eternal.

APPLICATION: The eternal sufferings of hell is a topic on which most people would rather not meditate, yet for weak, sin-inclined man this meditation is most profitable. The Holy Spirit counsels us through the Book of Ecclesiasticus (7:40): "Remember thy last end, and thou shalt never sin." Thus this parable was meant to induce us to consider the sad fate that awaits us if we fail to be numbered among the just on our judgment day.

We may be enclosed within the gospel net, but this does not automatically guarantee us eternal happiness. On the day of general judgment many souls that were signed with the sign of faith, many individuals who were washed with the saving waters of Baptism and had received the graces and aids of the other sacraments, will be numbered among the reprobate whose eternal lot will be the "furnace of fire." This is a sobering thought for even the most saintly.

Our Lord's statement that "there shall be weeping and gnashing of teeth" is not an exaggerated metaphor, as so many would wish, but a sober statement of fact by One who truly realized the full force of its meaning. Because He knew what the torments of the lost would be, He underwent the humiliations of the incarnation and the tortures of the crucifixion in order to save us from them. If Christ, the Son of God, Wisdom Incarnate, estimated the severity of eternal damnation to be such that no humiliation or pain He could endure here on earth was too much, can any Christian of sane mind make little of these torments or behave as if they didn't exist?

It is true that we cannot form an adequate image of eternal loss or of unending pain, but our intellects are capable, nevertheless, of forming a concept of their gravity sufficiently clear to move any wise man to do all in his power to avoid such a fate. Who is there among us who has not suffered some of the many pains, physical and mental, to which our human nature is subject? Broken limbs, burning fevers, frayed nerves, painful paralyses, yes, even the prosaic but torturing toothache. How eagerly we clutched at anything that offered relief or alleviation; how gladly we listened to the physician's cheering words that it would soon end, that the worst was over! What if these pains would never end, and if no relief or alleviation could ever be expected, and that there was not even a merciful death to put an end to this misery?

We have all, too, at one time or another, experienced the dreadful sense of loss when someone we dearly loved was taken from us. Yet through that mortal grief runs a thread of hope — the Christian guarantee that the separation is not really final — and also the certainty of experience that deep though our wound may be, the great healer, time, will, in due course, heal it. But how much greater would be our grief if we realized that this irrevocable separation was the result of our own free, deliberate will.

The damned will have a glimpse of the perfections of God at the particular judgment, and again at the general judgment. They will realize fully what they have lost — the one and only being that is capable of completely satisfying the innate desire of their souls. They will realize, too, that this source of perfect happiness is lost to them forever, but they will forever crave it with a longing that cannot be suppressed. Add to this perpetual and supreme frustration the positive sufferings caused by the "furnace of fire," and you can begin to understand why the saints of God trembled at the very mention of the word "hell."

And yet there are thousands of Christians today who are headed directly toward this fatal end. They have chosen the short cut of earthly pleasure and luxury which leads to eternal doom rather than the highroad of the commandments which ends in everlasting happiness. Like the rich man in the parable of Dives and Lazarus (p. 39), they will realize their folly only when it is too late, and like Dives they will try to offer the excuse that they hadn't sufficient warning of what awaited them. But they will be told that they had Moses and the prophets, nay, that they had more, for they had the very word of our Lord Himself repeated many times in His Gospel. No one who errs through invincible ignorance will be condemned to hell for his conduct, but no true Christian can claim invincible ignorance concerning his purpose in life and the means to attain it, and the dire consequences of his failure.

It is true also that the God of mercy sends repeated warnings to those who are on the downward path: "Is it my will that a sinner should die, saith the Lord God, and not that he should be converted from his ways, and live?" (Ez 18:23.) However, repeated refusals to hearken to these warnings can so deaden the conscience of the sinner that he will eventually fail to recognize them as warnings.

Lest that should happen to you, meditate on this parable. You are already safely in the gospel net if you have been baptized; you may at this moment be one of the fishes worthy of being rejected by the selecting angels; but, unlike the fishes in the real net, you can change your nature by sincere repentance, and become worthy to be welcomed by the Lord among "the blessed of his Father."

Who Are the Citizens of Christ's Kingdom?

While the rank-and-file Jews, especially the despised sinners and Publicans, eagerly listened to the preaching of Christ, and gradually rid themselves of their national prejudices, their leaders, the Scribes and Pharisees, set themselves against Him from the very beginning and remained immovable as granite in their opposition to Him. The Messias, to their minds, should mingle only with the elite of Israel, the strict observers of the letter of the law — themselves, in other words. But Christ consorted openly and freely with Publicans and sinners, and had in His inner circle ignorant fishermen of Galilee. He spoke of a kingdom based on humility, suffering, and universal brotherhood, while the Scribes and Pharisees expected a divinely established reign of earthly glory and world triumph for Israel. No wonder, therefore, that their innate personal and national pride prevented them from even attempting to understand Christ and His Gospel, and finally led them to the most disgraceful crime in history, the crucifixion on Calvary of this world's divine benefactor.

In the following four parables Christ tells the Scribes and Pharisees that they will exclude themselves from the heavenly kingdom to which they thought they had a prior and exclusive right, unless they accept His invitation to enter the kingdom of humility and self-abasement.

INVITATIONS TO A BANQUET

"The kingdom of heaven is likened to a king, who made a marriage for his son. And he sent his servants to call in them that were invited to the marriage;

and they would not come. Again he sent other servants, saying: Tell them that were invited, Behold, I have prepared my dinner; my beeves and fatlings are killed, and all things are ready: come ye to the marriage. But they neglected and went their ways, one to his farm, and another to his merchandise. And the rest laid hands on his servants, and having treated them contumeliously, put them to death. But when the king had heard of it, he was angry; and sending his armies, he destroyed those murderers, and burnt their city. Then he saith to his servants: The marriage indeed is ready, but they that were invited were not worthy. Go ye therefore into the highways, and as many as you shall find, call to the marriage. And his servants going forth into the ways, gathered together all that they found, both bad and good; and the marriage was filled with guests. And the king went in to see the guests: and he saw there a man who had not on a wedding garment. And he saith to him: Friend, how camest thou in hither not having a wedding garment? But he was silent. Then the king said to the waiters: Bind his hands and feet, and cast him into the exterior darkness: there shall be weeping and gnashing of teeth. For many are called, but few are chosen" (Mt 22:2–14).

EXPLANATION: The Jews as a whole, and the Pharisees especially, judged that, because the Messias was to come from their race, they were therefore assured not only of a place in His kingdom but the leading positions in it. This parable was intended to show them that because of their ungodliness, their pride, and their earthly attachments, they were about to forfeit not only all the privileges they hitherto had as God's chosen people on earth. But, worse still, they were to have no place in His heavenly kingdom because they willfully excluded themselves from the new Israel He was founding, the Church, which was to be the gateway to heaven (cf. Lk 14:16–24).

And to check any inclination to self-glory on the part of the sinners and Gentiles, "those from the highways and byways" who will supplant the Pharisees in the new kingdom, our Lord adds a warning on the necessity of proving oneself worthy of this great invitation, in the parable of the wedding garment.

The kingdom of heaven: For an explanation of this, see section one above.

A king, who made a marriage for his son: This was a very special celebration to which it was an honor to be invited. The king here is God the Father, the son is Christ, and the marriage is between Christ and His spouse, the Church.

Servants to call in them that were invited: The invitations had been sent out some time previously, and evidently had been accepted. But when the wedding day was at hand those invited refused to come. Ever since the call of Abraham (about 2000 B.C.; cf. Gn 18:18), the Jews had been called to the messianic kingdom. That call had been repeated by the Prophets and Sacred Writers of the Old Testament down through their history, but when Christ came "He came unto his own, and his own received him not" (Jn 1:11).

Again he sent other servants: With great forebearance the king overlooked the insult and tried once more to move them to a sense of propriety. The first servants were the Prophets, the second were the Apostles. These latter announced that the wedding feast was ready, the kingdom of God was at hand.

But they neglected and went their ways: Some of the invited just ignored the invitation, and went about their own personal affairs; they had no time for the king or his kingdom. Others were even worse; they maltreated the servants, and even put them to death. The Acts of the Apostles tell of the fulfillment of these words.

But when the king had heard of it: The murder of the servants did not go unpunished. The king sent his armies to destroy the murderers and burn their city. This prophecy of Christ, in the form of a parable, was fulfilled in the year A.D. 70, when Jerusalem was burned to the ground by the Romans under Titus.

They that were invited were not worthy: It was not the king who excluded them; they made themselves unworthy because of their worldliness and wickedness.

Into the highways . . . as many as you shall find: Since the elite of the city have excluded themselves, others must be found to fill the banquet chamber. Therefore the servants are told to go to the crossroads, very likely the roads leading from the country to the city, and bring in all they could find. These people would be unimportant, at least in the minds of the city magnates, country folk, strangers, and stragglers.

Gathered together . . . both bad and good: The king's messengers (the Apostles) went into the crossroads and byways of the pagan world, and announced the king's banquet (the founding of the Church). These people lis-tened and came gladly to the marriage feast. They accepted Christianity and became the chosen people instead of the Pharisees. As a result, "the marriage was filled with guests." We should note that it was God's plan to call the Gentiles to His Church no matter how the Pharisees reacted to His Gospel. Here the emphasis is on the rejection of the Pharisees and their supplanting by the despised Gentiles.

A man who had not on a wedding garment: According to most commentators on the Gospel this is a new parable, but one closely ·connected with the first, insofar as there were bad and good among those called from the crossroads. This second parable explains what will happen to the bad who are called and remain bad.

How camest thou . . . not having on a wedding garment? Evidently each guest was expected to wear a special, easily obtained, garment for the occasion; for if it had been difficult to obtain, the king would not have been angry with one who had been called in off the by-way. The lack of such a garment, therefore, showed a lack of respect and appreciation on the part of the delinquent.

But he was silent: The guilty one had no defense; his guilt was evident and inexcusable. Now the call to the Church given to the Gentiles is a tremendous privilege. And even if most of them were "bad," that is, entirely unworthy of such an honor, they could make themselves worthy, and many did. They could all easily obtain the wedding garment, the necessary grace, to make them acceptable to the Lord; but some failed in this. The mention of one unworthy person in the parable is taken to represent all failures. Numbers are used only to clarify the lesson intended.

Cast him into the exterior darkness: A wedding feast was no place for an improperly and disrespectfully dressed person. Heaven is not for those who have not made themselves worthy by penance and the acquisition of virtue. The binding of hands and feet signifies that there is no escape from the sentence of the king. The exterior darkness and the weeping and gnashing of teeth indicate the loss of happiness and the pain of damnation.

Many are called, but few are chosen: All get sufficient grace from God to attain to eternal salvation; but some, as is clear from the parable, fail to cooperate with the grace and are thus, through their own fault, excluded from the banquet of the "elect."

APPLICATION: How foolish the Pharisees were not to listen to our Lord's warnings. He gave them every opportunity of turning away from the false path their pride had chosen for them. His divine heart was ever ready to embrace them if only they would say mea culpa. "Jerusalem, Jerusalem, thou that killest the prophets, and stonest them that are sent unto thee, how often would I have gathered together thy children, as the hen doth gather her chickens under her wings, and thou wouldst not?" (Mt 23:37.) "God created us without our cooperation," says St. Augustine, "but He cannot save us unless we cooperate."

We too could make the Pharisees' mistake. We have the invitation to the wedding feast; in fact, we are already in the banquet hall, since our baptism; but are we wearing the wedding garment of virtue and grace? If not, we are no better off than those who rejected the invitation. The king may come in at any moment and cast out those who are not properly dressed. Being a member of the Church on earth is a wonderful privilege, and a sure guarantee that we will reach heaven, if we do what is expected of us. But the same obstacles which prevented the Pharisees from entering the kingdom — love of this world, its wealth and its pleasures — can impede us too, unless we are on our guard. The world with its allurements is very close to us; heaven seems very far away. Thus we must be prepared to do violence to our ordinary inclinations, to go against them whenever and wherever "the things that are Caesar's" tend to blot out or make us forget "the things that are God's."

This implies a daily carrying of the cross, a daily struggle against our evil inclinations, a daily endeavor to acquire true love of God and neighbor. This may sound superhuman, but Christ did not ask anyone to do the impossible. He led the way, and millions have followed Him to eternal glory. He has called us too and has placed within our easy reach in His Church all the grace we need. If we fail to use these divine helps, if we are found without the wedding garment, we will have no one to blame but ourselves. We have been called with the many. We can be among the "chosen."

THE TWO SONS
THE WICKED HUSBANDMEN

The following two parables were spoken by our Lord during the days that elapsed between Palm Sunday and Holy Thursday evening of the first Holy Week. During these four days, Jesus taught the people, cleansed the temple of the money-changers and merchants, wrought many miracles, and was sought eagerly by the crowds who had come up to the city for the approaching Passover. All this and the recent triumphal entry of Jesus into the city on the previous Sunday, greatly embittered His enemies, the chief priests and Pharisees. They had already planned to put Him to death (cf. Jn. 11:53), but the scenes they witnessed in Jerusalem during the past few days made it imperative for them to put their resolution into practice as soon as possible. Jesus knew their innermost thoughts and He not only exposed their plot, but the cause of it, namely, their hypocrisy, pride, and jealousy.

THE TWO SONS

"But what think you? A certain man had two sons; and coming to the first, he said: Son, go work today in my vineyard. And he answering, said: I will not. But afterwards, being moved with repentance, he went. And coming to the other, he said in like manner. And he answering, said: I go, Sir; and he went not. Which of the two did the father's will? They say to him: The first. Jesus saith to them: Amen I say to you, that the publicans and the harlots shall go into the kingdom of God before you. For John came to you in the way of justice, and you did not believe him. But the publicans and the harlots believed him: but you, seeing it, did not even afterwards repent, that you might believe him" (Mt 21:28–32).

EXPLANATION: The moral for the Pharisees here was very pointed. They looked down their noses at sinners, the publicans, and others whose occupations were far from respectable, and whose lives were not exactly blameless. These "sinners" were members of the chosen race, they had the law of Moses, but they were not remarkable for their observance of many of its precepts. They were called by God to work in His vineyard, to produce fruits worthy of heaven, but they had bluntly said no to that call. However, when John the Baptist announced the proximate arrival of the long-awaited Redeemer, and called on all to prepare for His coming by repenting of their sins, publicans and harlots and other despised sinners listened to the Baptist, repented, and followed Christ.

The Pharisees, on the other hand, like the second son in the parable, when called on to work in the vineyard, answered very promptly: "Yes, sir, we go," but they did not go. They kept the letter of the law in most things, but they did not keep its spirit. Their external observance, while not pleasing to God, did please their own pride. They sought the praise of men, not that of God. As our Lord Himself said of them, they left undone "the weightier things of the law; judgment, and mercy, and faith. . . . [they] strain out the gnat, and swallow the camel. . . . outwardly [they] . . . appear to men just; but inwardly . . . are full of hypocrisy and iniquity (Mt 23:23–28).

And our Lord left them no possibility of doubt as to the application of the lesson to themselves when He said: "Amen I say to you, the publicans and harlots are entering the kingdom of God before you." He does not say they are excluded by Him from the kingdom, but, so far, because of their refusal to repent, they have excluded themselves. The door of humble penance was still open to them, but the vast majority, alas, remained stubborn in their pride; they lost their earthly and their external kingdom.

APPLICATION: Although this parable was primarily intended to show up the hypocrisy of the Pharisees and the perilous position in which they stood in relation to God, it has a lesson and a warning against hypocrisy for all time. Lip service of God will not merit heaven. Nominal Christians are not working in the Lord's vineyard. At any moment they may be called to judgment, and what defense can they offer the just Judge? Will they even dare to offer the flimsy excuses with which they silence "the still voice of conscience" now: "We didn't realize how sinful we were"; "We were too occupied with family and personal cares to have time for our spiritual duties"; "We were led astray by the bad example of those around us"; "We didn't like to be different from others"; "We were going to put things right later"; "We didn't get a fair warning"? Who will dare to offer such excuses at the judgment seat of God? Their utter futility will then be apparent in all its nakedness.

The door of God's mercy is open to all who are still on this earth. The call to the Lord's vineyard is for all. If we said: "No, I will not go," we still have time to reverse that foolish decision. We can even blot out the useless pages of our life written to date by a generous giving of our whole selves to God's work from this moment onward. Remember the Publicans and harlots of this parable, the Matthews, the Mary Magdalenes, the Augustines, the Margarets of Cortona, the Matt Talbots, and the millions of unknown penitent saints in heaven — what God in His mercy did for them, He can do for you: He can make you a great saint in heaven.

If we answered the call to God's vineyard by accepting baptism and membership in His Church, but have grown lax in our fervor and refused to do the tasks allotted to us, we still have time, thanks to God's great patience, to put things right. Today I will look into my soul to see how much of my past life I have given to God, and how much I have kept for myself. If I were called on this moment to render an account to our Lord, would the balance sheet be in my favor? Is my corner of the vineyard producing abundant crops, or is it perhaps filling up with weeds and briars and brambles, producing nothing useful? If the latter is my case, then I'll say a heartfelt "Thank You, God, for not calling me to judgment today. I will begin right now to dig out these briars and brambles, so that my little corner of Your vineyard will be in good order when You do call me. With the help of Your divine grace, You shall find me working diligently in Your service when my cease-work call will come."

THE WICKED HUSBANDMEN

"Hear ye another parable. There was a man, an householder, who planted a vineyard, and made a hedge round about it, and dug in it a press, and built a tower, and let it out to husbandmen; and went into a strange country. And when the time of the fruits drew nigh, he sent his servants to the husbandmen that they might receive the fruits thereof. And the husbandmen laying hands on his servants, beat one, and killed another, and stoned another. Again he sent other servants more than the former; and they did to them in like manner. And last of all he sent to them his son, saying: They will reverence my son. But the husbandmen seeing the son, said among themselves: This is the heir: come, let us kill him, and we shall have his inheritance. And taking him, they cast him forth out of the vineyard, and killed him. When therefore the lord of the vineyard shall come, what will he do to those husbandmen? They say to him: He will bring those evil men to an evil end; and will let out his vineyard to other husbandmen that shall render him the fruit in due season. Jesus saith to them: Have you never read in the Scriptures: The stone which the builders rejected, the same is become the head of the corner? By the Lord this has been done; and it is wonderful in our eyes. Therefore I say to you, that the kingdom of God shall be taken from you, and shall be given to a nation yielding the fruits thereof. And whosoever shall fall on this stone, shall be broken: but on whomsoever it shall fall, it shall grind him to powder. And when the chief priests and Pharisees had heard his parables, they knew that he spoke of them" (Mt 21:33-45).

EXPLANATION: Having told the Pharisees in the preceding parable that they were disobedient children of God and would therefore have no part in their fathers' heritage, Christ now goes on to tell them in this parable that they are even worse than disobedient — they are rebels and murderers. They have in the past murdered the special messengers and prophets God has sent to them, up to and including John the Baptist. Now they have decided (cf. Jn 11:53) to put the only-begotten Son of God to death. Because of these heinous crimes, the vineyard of God, His kingdom on earth, would be taken from them and given to others "yielding the fruits thereof."

The vineyard as an image of God's kingdom on earth occurs frequently in the Old Testament (cf. Ps 79:8–16; Is 5:1–7; 27:1–7; Jer 2:21). God identified His vineyard with the Chosen People, "for the vineyard of the Lord of hosts is the house of Israel: and the man of Juda, his pleasant plant" (Is 5:7), and the leaders of the Chosen People especially were the husbandmen who were given care of this vineyard. The Pharisees, therefore, could not fail to understand the meaning of our Lord's words.

Made a hedge round about it: The owner of the vineyard did all that was necessary to ensure a good harvest — the hedge was needed to keep out robbers, animal and human; the press was necessary to crush the grapes at harvesttime; the tower was used to house the watchmen who guarded the vineyard day and night during the grape-picking season. In other words, the owner handed over a perfect vineyard to the husbandmen. He had every reason to expect a good return. A glance through the history of the Chosen People from the day Abraham was called out of Ur of the Chaldees to the coming of Christ will show how lavishly God showered gifts on Israel, His vineyard, during those two thousand years. And what return did He receive — let our Savior's parable be the answer.

The time of fruits drew nigh: Autumn.

He sent his servants: To collect the wine or the value thereof. Thus would any reasonable master of a vineyard act. God, as Master of the Chosen People,

sent His servants, the prophets, generation after generation, calling on His people to produce fruits of penance, to turn to God with a sincere heart and to prepare themselves for the coming Redeemer.

The husbandmen laying hands on his servants, beat one, and killed another, and stoned another: Instead of paying the debts they owed to their master, they maltreated the innocent messengers. This is exactly what the leaders of the Jews did to God's messengers. Because their pride and hardness of heart would not let them repent of their sins, they could not bear to hear God's words of reproach, and so they silenced God's mouthpieces by torture and death (cf. Neh 9; Acts 8:51–54).

And last of all he sent to them his son: The owner of the vineyard rightly expected that the wicked tenants would respect his son, even though they had not respected his servants. But he did not realize how steeped in wickedness these tenants were.

The husbandmen seeing the son . . . let us kill him: On seeing the son and heir of the owner arrive, these sinful tenants formed a most unjust plot; they decided to kill the heir and thus rid themselves of all further reminders of their iniquity and so possess in peace, they thought, the property they had obtained from murder and injustice.

God, the owner of Israel's vineyard, had no doubts as to the reception and treatment His only Son would receive from His tenants. Yet in His infinite mercy He gave them this last opportunity to atone for their past sins. Our Lord Himself was now telling these tenants, the Pharisees and Scribes, that He was the Son of God; that He knew what they have planned to do with Him. But they did not listen to His entreaties, they had their hearts set on being free from any master, and of being owners, not tenants, of the divine vineyard, and so they carried out their perfidious plans a few days later.

Cast him forth out of the vineyard: The tenants of the parable cast the son out of his vineyard, thus claiming it as their own, and then they put him to death. This is exactly what the tenants of God's vineyard did. They had Christ, the Son of God, condemned to die on the cross — a death reserved for the vilest criminals and the outcasts of society. The execution took place on the hill outside the holy city of God, Jerusalem.

When therefore the lord of the vineyard shall come: Christ now asks His hearers what they think the owner of the vineyard will do to the wicked tenants. They answer rightly that these tenants will receive a just punishment for their crimes, and that the vineyard will be given to other tenants who will carry out the owner's will. It is likely this answer was given by the disciples and some of the God-fearing Jews who were also present, and not given by the Pharisees, who in Lk 20:16 say: "God forbid" when they hear it, for they evidently realize it applies to themselves.

Have you never read in the Scriptures: Any slight doubt there may have been in the minds of the Pharisees that the parable applied to themselves is removed by these words our Lord added. He quotes two verses of Psalm 117: "The stone which the builders rejected; the same is become the head of the corner. This is the Lord's doing: and it is wonderful in our eyes." By applying these words to Himself, our Lord is telling the Pharisees that He will be the strength and source of stability and unity between the various races of whom His new kingdom will be built, while He will be a cause of destruction and dismay to all those who so scornfully and sinfully reject Him.

Whosoever shall fall on this stone, shall be broken: but on whomsoever it shall fall, it shall grind him to powder: (Cf. Is 8:14; Dn 2:44).

And when the chief priests and Pharisees: There was no mistaking His meaning; they knew it was of themselves he was speaking, but, instead of beating their breasts and repenting, they only became more determined in their opposition and would have laid hands on Him there and then but they feared the crowd.

APPLICATION: There are two leading thoughts that come to the mind of any true believer on hearing this parable: the infinite patience and mercy of God in dealing with mankind, and the unsounded depths of wickedness and ingratitude to which men can sink. The words of Christ in this parable were fulfilled to the last letter in those Jewish leaders to whom He spoke that first Holy Week. To them God had given a fully equipped vineyard: His revelation, His protection, His promises of future redemption and eternal happiness. All He asked in return was their cooperation. But they had other plans; they wanted their heaven on earth. Yet God was patient with them; He sent prophet after prophet to recall them to their senses, but they maltreated these messengers of God and sometimes even put them to death. Finally He sent His only beloved Son in human nature to soften those hard hearts and bring them a final offer of His forgiveness and pardon. But, instead of accepting this offer of mercy, they only made it an occasion for an even greater sin. To their other crimes of murder and injustice they added the crime of deicide. This is surely the blackest page of history human nature has written.

Yet God's infinite mercy and goodness triumphed over men's lowest and darkest wickedness — the Savior's death on Calvary redeemed the human race, the sons of Adam rallied around the standard of Christ, and a new vineyard was set up for mankind. The synagogue was replaced by the church; the Chosen People gave way to the Christians; the children of Abraham were replaced by the children of God. Therefore while we grieve from the depths of our hearts over the heinous crime of our fellow men, we can rejoice that God has been infinitely merciful to us. He has made us members of His Church; He has opened heaven for us and has left all the aids and means we need for our journey thither.

Are we grateful to our divine Benefactor; are we devoted children of our heavenly Father; are we, at this moment, on the road to heaven, bearing the crosses of our state of life bravely and cheerfully? If our conscience says "yes," then a heartfelt "thank You" to our Savior; if the answer is "no," then let us be up and doing today; tomorrow may be too late.

Earthly Versus Heavenly Wisdom

Our Lord, because He was divine, knew our human nature infinitely better than we can ever come to know it. He knew that of the multitudes of all generations who would become His followers and who would gladly have heaven as their eternal abode, many will fail or be strongly tempted to fail because of the hold which earthly things have on their bodies. As surely as the law of gravity attracts our human bodies to the earth and holds them there unless and until the higher power within us commands these bodies to move, so likewise does this world attract and hold captive not only the body but the spirit of man unless his higher self decrees otherwise. This resistance to a natural attraction calls for self-denial and self-mortification, occupations by no means attractive to the natural man. But, just as in battle the weary soldier is sustained in his struggle by the thought of victory and urged on to renewed efforts by the fear of the consequences of defeat, so too, the soldier of Christ is sustained by the thought of the eternal reward which will follow from his efforts and is moved to put forth ever greater efforts because of the dire results which failure will inevitably produce. When eternity is at stake, what are a few years of sacrifice? When the odds are a certain thousand to one, who would grudge the one?

It was for this reason Christ frequently emphasized the need for detachment from material things, and stressed the incomparable value of the heavenly reward.* In the following three parables this teaching is put vividly before the minds of His hearers. In the first two, the sad end of two men who allowed worldly goods and pleasures to chain them to earth, is depicted in language no one can misinterpret. The third parable is a call to His followers to exercise at least as much zeal in acquiring heavenly riches as the wicked and foolish show in their acquisition of earthly treasures.

---

* See p. 10; also Mt 12:20–46; Mk 9:42; Lk 12:23; 18:18.

THE RICH FOOL

"And he spoke a similitude to them, saying: The land of a certain rich man brought forth plenty of fruits. And he thought within himself, saying: What shall I do, because I have no room where to bestow my fruits? And he said: This will I do: I will pull down my barns and will build greater; and into them will I gather all things that are grown to me, and my goods. And I will say to my soul: Soul, thou hast much goods laid up for many years, take thy rest; eat, drink, make good cheer. But God said to him: Thou fool, this night do they require thy soul of thee: and whose shall those things be which thou hast provided? So is he that layeth up treasure for himself, and is not rich towards God" (Lk 12:16–21).

EXPLANATION: The setting for this parable is as follows: immense crowds had gathered about Jesus "so that they trod one upon another" (Lk 12:1), and He was instructing them. The subject of His teaching was that it was the life of the soul that really mattered; the short life of the body on earth was very unimportant when compared with the immortal life hereafter. Trials and persecutions would come upon His faithful followers on earth, but when compared with the unending tortures of hell they were as nothing. Their merciful loving Father would see them safely through their earthly trials if they remained faithful to Him. "Be not afraid of them who kill the body, and after that have no more that they can do. But I will show you whom you shall fear: fear ye him, who after he hath killed, hath power to cast into hell. . . . Are not five sparrows sold for two farthing, and not one of them is forgotten before God? Yea, the very hairs of your head are all numbered. Fear not therefore: you are of more value than many sparrows" (Lk 12:4–7).

In the midst of this discourse on the relative importance of earthly and heavenly wealth, a man in the crowd, whose thoughts are steeped in worldly concerns, and on whom the discourse is lost, appeals to Christ to tell his brother to divide the inheritance with him. The man's thoughts are "of the earth" — earthly. He has no time for things spiritual at present, his elder brother has evidently refused to give him his share of the deceased father's property; the man's claim may be just, the brother's action may be just; there is, however, dishonesty or covetousness in one or the other, but the man thinks Christ should take his side, and make the elder brother hand over the disputed property. Christ refused, saying: "Man, who has appointed me a judge or arbitrator over you?" It was not His mission to settle temporal disputes or arbitrate in secular matters, but from this interruption, unseemly and untimely as it was, He took the occasion to warn His audience against covetousness, the overeagerness for earthly goods. "Take heed," He said, "and guard yourselves from all covetousness, for a man's life does not consist in the abundance of his possessions." The true life, the everlasting life, is not bought with earthly goods; in fact the man who is covetous of these earthly possessions and devotes all his energies to acquiring them puts himself in the immediate danger of losing his eternal life. To bring out this point He proposed the above parable or story of a foolish man who forfeited the eternal happiness of heaven because of his inordinate attachment to the goods of earth.

The land of a certain rich man brought forth plenty of fruits: There is no question here of ill-gotten goods. This landowner was blessed "with a rich yield from his field." In this there was no fault; his wealth presumably came to him without injury or injustice to any of his neighbors. But his fault lay in his failure to recognize that this abundance was not for his ruin, but for his salvation, that it was given him not to satisfy his unruly desire for wealth, but to offer him an occasion for unselfish generosity.

What shall I do . . . I have no room where to bestow my fruits? His dilemma is caused by utter selfishness. His one and only thought is to keep all these good things for himself. His storehouses were already full, yet his hungry soul felt it needed more. His question was well answered by St. Ambrose: "Thou hast barns — the bosoms of the needy, the houses of the widows, the mouths of orphans and of infants," but such a solution of his problem never entered the self-centered mind of this covetous man.

I will pull down my barns and build greater: His solution is in keeping with his selfish nature. He will put himself to a lot of trouble and waste some of his wealth rather than give any of it away. In the new larger barn he will store all his produce and goods, and then he will say to his soul:

Soul, thou hast much goods laid up for many years: There is sad irony in this, that it is to his soul he addresses himself. To that soul which is immortal and destined for an eternity of happiness, he now announces that it should content itself and be happy with a few earthly trinkets.

Take thy rest; eat, drink, make good cheer: The pleasures and comforts of the body are the be-all and the end-all of this man's desires. Having laid aside all the needs and luxuries his body desires for many years to come, he foolishly thinks his cup of happiness is filled to the brim. But, full of worldly wisdom and prudence though he is, he acts most foolishly in forgetting that his body is mortal. And just when he is congratulating himself on his good fortune in having so wisely provided for himself, the hand of God is grasping the shears to sever the man's life thread.

God said to him: Thou fool, this night do they require thy soul of thee: A strong term, but a true one; God does not call people or things by the wrong name. Fool he was, in the strictest meaning of the word, and he himself will be the first to admit it. He had devoted his life's work to amassing earthly goods which he must suddenly leave, and he is entering a new world, the world of the spirit, empty-handed and utterly unprepared. In his preoccupation with the things of earth he has completely forgotten heaven, he never gave a thought to the donor of all goods, and now he is called to meet that donor face to face to render an account of his life's work.

And whose shall those things be which thou has provided? To add vinegar to his already bitter cup, the fruits of his years of labor in which he had set his heart are now an added source of regret and self-condemnation. He has to part with them as if he never owned them; their memory will be but a bitter reminder of his life's folly.

So is he that layeth up treasure for himself, and is not rich towards God: Our Lord Himself applies the parable. He exhorts His hearers not to imitate this foolish man in the story and give all their time and energy to gathering this world's goods, or their fate will be like that of the foolish man; but rather should they strive to store up for themselves spiritual treasures which will make them "rich towards God," that is, treasures that will earn for them admission into the heavenly mansions when the Master calls them to the judgment seat.

APPLICATION: The lesson which our divine Lord teaches us in this parable is obvious to all, and it is perhaps as difficult to put into practice as it is obvious. To be in this world and not of it, to collect the necessary goods of this world by honest labor and yet remain detached from them, to possess and not be possessed by worldly riches, this is something to which our weak nature responds very reluctantly. But as Christians we should and do know that the road Christ mapped out for us in order to reach heaven was not a path of roses but the way of the cross. "If any man will come after me, let him deny himself, take up his cross, and follow me" (Mt 16:24). Had there been an easier way, the good, kindhearted Savior would have pointed it out. However, there is but the one: the rugged rock-strewn road to Calvary. A large percentage of Christians clearly understand this. Many renounce their right to possess even the necessary things of life by taking on themselves the vows of religion, trusting in God to provide for them — a trust which has never failed — and thus setting themselves free to devote their whole time and energies to the service of God and neighbor. Others, and they are of necessity the more numerous, have to possess and use the world's goods in order to provide bodily sustenance for themselves and their dependents, but while so doing they never let their temporal possessions come between them and their God. To do this is not easy, but God's helping grace is always available to the willing heart.

But there is still a third group, those who follow the foolish man described in the parable. Like him they are so enmeshed and ensnared in their desire to collect good things for the body that they forget that that body is mortal and will have to go naked into the grave very soon. They may not have large barns bursting at the seams with the fruits of their fields, but, large or small, they have allowed these possessions to become the prison houses of their hearts and their thought. In their mad rush for earthly treasures they have given themselves no time to stop and think of the real important fact in life, namely, that soon they must leave this world and all it holds dear to them.

Departure from this world is not to be feared; rather, the arrival at another for which they had made no preparation. That other world of which they had often heard, but which they shrugged off as something fit for the weak-minded, will now open before them in all its awe-inspiring immensity; they will have a momentary glimpse of the eternal beauty and happiness they lost for "a mess of pottage" before they enter the unending valley of sorrow which they elected for themselves when they chose earthly baubles instead of God during their period of trial here below.

This has been the fate of many foolish men and women in the past; this will be the fate of many more in the future. It could be my fate too, unless I be ever on the alert to keep myself free from the snares of worldly wealth. And I must remember, it is not the quantity of this world's goods which I hold that will be my undoing, but the quality of the hold they have on me. The fate of the rich man in the parable need not, and should not, be mine.

DIVES AND LAZARUS

"There was a certain rich man, who was clothed in purple and fine linen, and feasted sumptuously every day. And there was a certain beggar named Lazarus, who lay at his gate, full of sores, desiring to be filled with the crumbs that fell from the rich man's table, and no one did give him; moreover the dogs came, and licked his sores. And it came to pass that the beggar died, and was carried by angels into Abraham's bosom. And the rich man also died: and he was buried in hell. And lifting up his eyes when he was in torments, he saw Abraham afar off, and Lazarus in his bosom: and he cried, and said: Father Abraham, have mercy on me, and send Lazarus that he may dip the tip of his finger in water, to cool my tongue: for I am tormented in this flame. And Abraham said to him: Son, remember that thou didst receive good things in thy lifetime, and likewise Lazarus evil things, but now he is comforted and thou art tormented. And besides all this, between us and you there is fixed a great chaos: so that they who would pass from hence to you, cannot, nor from thence come hither. And he said: Then, father, I beseech thee, that thou wouldst send him to my father's house, for I have five brethren, that he may testify unto them, lest they also come into this place of torments. And Abraham said to him: They have Moses and the prophets; let them hear them. But he said: No, father Abraham: but if one went to them from the dead, they will do penance. And he said to him: If they hear not Moses and the prophets, neither will they believe if one rise again from the dead" (Lk 16:19-31).

EXPLANATION: In the parable of the unjust steward the lesson taught was that the seekers after eternal life must be prepared to exercise such zeal and fervor in their search for it, as the children of this world expend in providing worldly goods for themselves.

The parable of Dives and Lazarus brings out this point very forcefully by placing before our eyes two individuals whose state, both in this life and the next, is diametrically opposed. A rich man had all the wealth of this world his heart could desire, and the enjoyment of this wealth seemed his sole purpose in life. Here is a man whose cup of happiness is full to overflowing, and who is the very model of human contentment. At the rich man's gate lay one who was at the other end of the social scale, a beggar whose sole earthly possessions were rags and ulcers. He was the embodiment of earthly misery and misfortune.

The scene changes, both men die, and the rich man has entered into an eternity of suffering and torments, the poor man into communion with the blessed in Abraham's bosom, enjoying eternal happiness. The rich man calls on his father Abraham for succor, but is told the time for pleading is over. The curtain drops and the moral is evident: he who serves mammon in this life is preparing for himself an unhappy eternity. While he who serves God faithfully in this world can look forward confidently to a happy future life.

There was a certain rich man: His name is not given by Christ, whereas He tells us the name of the beggar as if to reverse this world's values. Among men the names of the rich are revered and remembered; those of the poor and lowly are not even worth recording. The name Dives by which this man is commonly known today is simply the Latin word for "rich man."

Clothed in purple and fine linen: The most expensive apparel of that time, available to princes and men of great wealth only.

Feasted sumptuously every day: His was the life of the idle rich, whose sole purpose in life was to cram as much earthly pleasure and luxury as possible into each day.

A certain beggar named Lazarus: His name means "God is my help" or "May God be my help," and it was surely symbolic when given to this poor beggar. To relieve themselves of the burden of providing for a cripple, the family would send him, or, if he were unable to walk, carry him, each day and place him at some vantage point, on a busy street corner, at one of the temple gates, or near the principal entrance of a rich man's home. The few pennies and the few crumbs of bread received would enable the cripple to eke out a miserable existence. Lazarus, covered with sores which his scanty clothing was unable to hide or protect from the elements or even from stray dogs, and evidently unable to walk, was "cast down" (as the original Greek signifies) each morning by his relatives or friends, who were glad to wash their hands of him for the day.

Desiring to be filled with the crumbs that fell from the rich man's table: Here, surely, Lazarus could, with all confidence, get more than enough to keep soul and body together. Dives had a superabundance of this world's goods. An occasional soiled tunic or slightly worn mantle would not be much to expect from the wardrobe of one who dressed as Dives did. Among the hired helpers of such a household there must have been many who could and would give a helping hand to Lazarus to bathe and bandage his sores, if only the master said the word; but that word was never uttered, the soiled tunic was never given. Lazarus got some crumbs, otherwise he would not have been placed at the same gate each day, but this could hardly be called generosity, much less charity, on the part of Dives.

Moreover the dogs came, and licked his sores: Dives passed him by several times each day without casting even a compassionate glance in his direction; most likely he averted his gaze lest the sight of that repulsive beggar might upset his refined instincts. The dogs of the neighborhood, dumb beasts though they were, showed more compassion or at least more curiosity. Lazarus was evidently so helpless that he was unable to drive the dogs away.

It came to pass that the beggar died: Death came at last, a welcome release from his life of misery, a life borne, it is understood from the sequel, with resignation and patience. And as he lived, unwanted and unsought after, he died unmourned, for his funeral is not even mentioned. Probably Dives ordered his servants to cast the body in a pauper's grave, if not out of respect for the body of a fellow man at least out of consideration for his own health and well-being.

And was carried by the angels into Abraham's bosom: The soul of Lazarus leaves the rag-covered ulcerous body only to find itself carried by angels into the happy abode of the just. As a child of Abraham, the father of the Jews, Lazarus is welcomed with joy into the bosom of the great patriarch. As heaven was not reopened until the death of Christ, the souls of the just had to wait in limbo until that great day arrived. Note that the parable continues to describe Lazarus and Dives in the afterdeath scene as if they had already received their resurrected bodies.

And the rich man also died: and was buried in hell: Notwithstanding the luxury of delicate food and fine clothing with which Dives pampered his body, he yet had to go the way of all flesh. The burial of Dives is not mentioned, but it was the last pompous display of worldly wealth and power as far as he was concerned. No doubt all the wealthy neighbors and friends turned out, and the hired mourners chanted his praises and extolled his virtues.

And lifting up his eyes: And while these vain empty honors were being bestowed on his dead body, Dives' soul had already faced the just Judge and had been found wanting. The fearful sentence was passed: "Depart from me ye cursed, into the everlasting flames prepared for the devil and his angels." His eternal torments had begun long before the hired mourners had ended singing his false praises at the graveside on earth.

He saw Abraham afar off, and Lazarus in his bosom: Dives was permitted to see the happiness which his folly had lost for him. He too could have been in Abraham's bosom, where Lazarus was, instead of in the place of "torments." One of the principal causes of the sufferings of the damned will be the "pain of loss," the full realization of what they have lost and that this loss is utterly and entirely their own fault.

And he cried, and said: Father Abraham: Abraham was the father of the Chosen People. Every Jew was proud of his great ancestor, and gloried in his descent from this close friend of God. Unfortunately the Jews put too much reliance on their carnal descent from the patriarch, and many failed to emulate their father's virtues (cf. Mt 3:9; Jn 8:39–41; Rom 2:17–29). Dives' confidence in his descent from Abraham is so great that even now, although a convicted delinquent, he appeals to his "father" as if he had been a loyal son all his years on earth. He does not ask for much, it is true, all he asks is:

Send Lazarus that he may dip the tip of his finger in water, to cool my tongue: for I am tormented in this flame: He who in his lifetime had but to snap his fingers and a host of servants supplied all the desires of his palate — the most exquisite food and the costliest wines — does not now dare to ask for a drink of water to quench his thirst, but would deem it the greatest favor if the tip of his tongue could be touched by a finger dipped in cool water! And he asks that Lazarus should favor him by performing this act of mercy for him. Lazarus whom he had ignored and neglected on earth. Lazarus whose patient look and silent plea for a little mercy had gone unheeded. Lazarus whose burning sores and parched palate never cost him a thought in his days of opulence. This Lazarus is now in a position to be his benefactor, he thinks, and he dares to ask this favor of him.

Son, remember that thou didst receive good things in thy lifetime, and likewise Lazarus evil things: Abraham gives him the honored title of "son," but the time has passed when that privilege could have helped Dives. During his earthly career he had completely failed to live up to his title as son of Abraham, and through Abraham of adopted son of God. Lazarus on the other hand had served God in life, bearing patiently the afflictions and crosses his loving father had allotted him. And now he is to enjoy an unending life of happiness.

And between us and you there is fixed a great chaos: Dives evidently did not question the justice or the immutability of the sentence. All he hoped for was a slight alleviation of the torment, but Abraham tells him that even this little he cannot expect. The time for succor and mercy is over.

And he said: Then, father, I beseech thee that thou wouldst send him to my father's house: Having failed to get any smallest relief from his own torments, Dives now remembers the five brothers who are still on earth, and who evidently are leading the same worldly life that he had lived. He asks now that Lazarus should go back from the dead to warn them of what will be their eternal fate if they continue their godless mode of living. This request is put into the mouth of Dives by our Lord in order to emphasize the point made by Abraham in his answer, and so the question raised by theologians as to whether a damned soul could desire the salvation of others hardly arises. There is more than a veiled hint at self-justification on the part of Dives in his request. He implies that his brothers would be converted from their sinful ways if somebody returned from the dead to warn them, and thereby hints that he and they had not sufficient proof from God as to the existence of a future life and the necessity of providing for it.

They have Moses and the prophets: Abraham's answer is curt and almost stern. The excuse brought forward by Dives is a false one. He did know that this life was but a preparation for the eternal life; he did know what road to follow in order to gain heaven. God in His mercy had clearly revealed to the Chosen People all that was necessary for them to earn eternal life. The law of Moses and the prophets was the clearly marked road map to heaven issued by God to the children of Abraham. If they refused to follow it, as Dives had done, and as his brothers were doing, they had no one but themselves to blame.

No, father Abraham, but if one went to them from the dead they will do penance: Against the emphatic declaration of Abraham whom he calls "father," Dives insists that the revelation God has given is not enough for his brothers, as it was not enough for him.

Ordinary folk may find sufficient grounds for faith and fidelity to God in the inspired books, but men of wealth and standing require, and in fact demand, a lot more. If God does not take their superior nature into account, all the worse for God! How like today's self-styled intelligentsia. How like the priests and scribes on Calvary: "If he be the king of Israel, let him now come down from the cross, and we will believe him" (Mt 27:42). He did something more than this, He came out alive from the sealed tomb on the third day, and yet they did not believe. This was a clear proof of the truth of Abraham's next words:

If they hear not Moses and the prophets, neither will they believe if one rise again from the dead: If they ignore God's gift of revelation, if they fail to use the road map to heaven which He has so mercifully given to them, they have no right to expect extraordinary aids from God. A messenger from the dead is wholly unnecessary for those who accept God's revelation; he is entirely useless to those who do not.

APPLICATION: If it were anyone else but Christ who had said: "You cannot serve God and mammon," we might feel inclined to argue about the truth of the statement. Seen in the supernatural light of eternity, the statement of course is self-evident, but the crude naked fact is that so few of us mortals, earthbound as we are, can see things in their supernatural setting. While no man of sound mind will question the truth that his earthly sojourn is of very short duration, and that he will have to leave it relatively soon, the vast majority act as if they had a permanent home here on earth. And this is true not only of those who try (ineffectively, perhaps) to blot out from their minds all thought of the future life, but even of those who openly profess Christianity and who recite daily: "I believe in the resurrection of the body, and the life everlasting."

Dives' folly consisted in this: he was so fully occupied with enjoying the goods of this world that he had no time for God, for his neighbor, or for his immortal soul. He admits in his second request to Abraham that he had paid no heed to the warnings given in revelation, and in natural reason for that matter, that man's end is not to be found in the pleasures and comforts of the body, but is to be sought in a future life through the faithful observance of the natural and revealed law during this life. Instead, he ignored God and his own true welfare by making himself a slave of mammon and now, too late, he sees his folly. It was not because he was rich that he had merited eternal torment, but because he let his riches become his master and his god. Forgetting the love he owed to God and neighbor — the essence of the whole law and the prophets — he lived a life of selfishness on this earth, serving only his own lower self, and only in death did he see life for the first time in its true perspective. Lazarus, on the other hand, did not get to the abode of the just because he was poor and afflicted, but because he accepted his poverty and his afflictions patiently and submissively from the hand of God. He accepted life for what it is, a period of trial and preparation in which to earn an eternal existence. Death for him was the beginning of happiness. For Dives it was the end.

God forbid that we should ever be guilty of such a crime against God and against our own eternal interests. This parable was spoken by Christ and preserved in the inspired Gospel just for this purpose, to help you avoid such a fatal mistake. If, like Dives, you have some of this world's goods, use them to help you on the road to heaven, don't let them become fetters which will chain you to earth. On all sides of you there are Lazaruses placed there by God to give you the opportunity to exercise fraternal charity. Be a true brother to them now and you will not have to envy their lot in the hereafter. If on the other hand your lot on earth is that of a Lazarus, the lot of the many for whom this life is one long struggle with poverty, disease, hardships, and disappointments, remember the saying: "The disciple is not above the master." Our Lord willingly chose poverty and suffering for His lot in order to set us an example. Remember every step patiently and willingly taken on your hard path of life is a step nearer to the end of your sufferings and the beginning of your eternal happiness.

THE UNJUST STEWARD

"And he said also to his disciples: There was a certain rich man who had a steward: and the same was accused unto him that he had wasted his goods. And he called him, and said to him: How is it that I hear this of thee? give an account of thy stewardship: for now thou canst be steward no longer. And the steward said within himself: What shall I do, because my lord taketh away from me the stewardship? To dig I am not able; to beg I am ashamed. I know what I will do, that when I am removed from the stewardship, they may receive me into their houses. Therefore calling together every one of his lord's debtors, he said to the first: How much dost thou owe my lord? But he said: a hundred barrels of oil. And he said to him: Take thy bill and sit down quickly, and write fifty. Then he said to another: And how much dost thou owe? Who said: A hundred quarters of wheat. He said to him: Take thy bill and write eighty. And the lord commended the unjust steward, forasmuch as he had done wisely: for the children of this world are wiser in their generation than the children of light" (Lk 16:1-8).

EXPLANATION: The purpose of this parable was to stress the lesson that in striving to reach heaven we must use all our wisdom and our prudence. If a man has enough foresight to provide a living for himself in this life, surely he should have more foresight to provide for the life which will last forever.

A certain rich man who had a steward: It was the common practice of the time for the wealthy to entrust the management of their property to an agent. This agent was allowed a lot of freedom, but it was understood that he should always work for the master's interests. Such a steward or manager was somewhat more than a servant; he held a position of honor. It was his duty to manage all the master's business affairs: to let the land, the orchards, and olive groves; to collect the annual rents which were generally paid in kind; to sell the produce thus collected in the market or to other tenants; to pay all the running expenses and hand the annual surplus over to his master.

He had wasted his goods: News was brought to this particular master that his steward was not as loyal as he should be, that he was living too sumptuously at his master's expense, was making some foolish speculations or perhaps selling his master's property to his relatives and friends at a bargain price. It does not seem from the story that he was putting aside any of his master's money for his own use later on, as he seems to have had nothing saved for the future when his dismissal came.

How is it that I hear this of thee? Give an account: The master asked for an explanation, but none was forthcoming, for evidently the steward realized there was no defense he could offer. He brought the books up to date and handed them over to the master.

And the steward said within himself: He realized the predicament in which his evildoings had placed him, and sat down to think of the best way out of his difficulty.

To dig I am not able; to beg I am ashamed: He sees clearly that because of his dishonesty any hope of getting employment as a steward in another household is out of the question. His easy life as a steward leaves him unprepared to take up any employment which involves hard labor. And begging is out of the question.

I know . . . receive me into their houses: His dishonest mind finds a clever but dishonest solution.

His lord's debtors: The master in question was either a landlord whose tenants paid him in kind each year; therefore in bad seasons they would naturally fall behind in their payments, and thus were in debt to their landlord. Or he was a dealer in farm products, and had given credit to some of his customers. The steward would naturally know all about these affairs — it was he who would keep the accounts and make the deals. He now decides to provide for his future by dishonestly buying the favor and indebtedness of these people with his master's property.

Take thy bill . . . and write fifty: He reduces the debt with the connivance of the debtors, and therefore they must befriend him, both out of gratitude for the dishonest favor and for fear of blackmail.

And the lord commended the unjust steward: The employer, though defrauded of his property, could not but admire the worldly if dishonest wisdom of the steward. He had lost his position through dishonesty; now he had provided for his future by another clever act of dishonesty.

This verse has caused difficulty to many readers, who thought the master who commended the unjust steward was our Lord. It is not our Lord, but the employer, who "commended," that is, admired the astuteness of his dishonest employee. The employer did not approve certainly of his property's being thus dishonestly squandered, but he did admire the worldly wisdom of the steward.

For the children of this world: Our

Lord now applies the lesson of the parable. The "children of this world" are those whose sole interest is centered on the pleasures and wealth of this world, and "the children of light" are those who are striving to merit eternal life. The conclusion and the lesson our Lord wishes His followers to draw from the parable of the unjust steward is that they should imitate his prudence in providing for their eternal future. The question has been asked, why did our Lord pick as an example of prudence one who was an unscrupulous swindler? The material settings of all our Lord's parables are taken from the daily life and occurrences of His time. That a steward of the caliber here described could be found in many parts of Palestine at that time is more than likely. His dishonesty is clearly disapproved of when he is called the unjust steward.

APPLICATION: We are Christians, followers of Christ, because we know He is the Way, the Truth, and the Life. He is the Way that leads to heaven; He is the eternal Truth who teaches us how to reach heaven; He is the Author of life, of life in this world and of eternal life. We know all this, and we are sincere when we say that we want and intend to get to heaven; but when it comes to practice, when it comes to taking the necessary steps to get there, how effective is our intention?

This is a question I could ask myself in all sincerity today. This is the very question our Lord asks me in the parable I have just read. And to help me answer the question, He suggests that I compare my zeal and sincerity in working for my eternal salvation with the zeal and sincerity of those whose sole interest in life is to get its pleasures and its wealth.

Now out of my free fifty-six hours each week, after deducting eight hours for sleep and eight hours for work each day, how many of them do I devote to acquiring heaven? Am I one of those who thinks that when he has spent one half hour at Sunday Mass and ten minutes each day for daily prayers he has done enough to earn heaven? Am I one of those who cannot possibly spare a half hour for daily Mass each morning or fifteen minutes for evening devotions? When asked to join some sodality or some Catholic action group, is the excuse that I am too busy with the affairs of the family really valid? The keen businessman, with all his busy hours finds time to read literature that helps his purpose in life, yet I, with all the free hours at my disposal, hardly ever read any books or magazines that would help me get a deeper knowledge of God and the eternal truths.

Most Catholics leave these things to religious, nuns, and priests, as if they themselves were not on the way to heaven, and did not need to use every help they can get on the way. God expects lay people to provide for the bodily upkeep of themselves and their families, and He will count that as time served in acquiring heaven, if done with the right intention; but here we are interested in the time wasted on idle conversation or, worse still, on sinful amusements.

We are stewards of God's gifts. He has given us gifts of body and soul to use according to His intentions. We can squander these gifts or we can use them honestly and profitably for God and for ourselves. The day of reckoning is near to all of us, nearer by far than any of us would want to believe. We will be called on then to render an account of our stewardship. But we have time to put our accounts in order. We can erase all our past mistakes and dishonest figures in a sincere confession and we can start a new, clean, straight, and upright set of figures which we can fearlessly produce at the judgment seat.

A few moments of silent pondering here and now on this all-important matter will be the most profitable moments I have spent this week.

Active Vigilance in God's Service

As we saw in the preceding parables, detachment from earthly goods and pleasures is a virtue absolutely necessary for those who wish to gain eternal life. But it is only the first step on the road. It is but the digging out of the weeds and brambles. The garden must then be planted, watered, and constantly cared for if the gardener wishes to have a worthwhile harvest. The sincere Christian must therefore not only detach himself from worldly entanglements, but he must especially attach himself to the things of God; that is, he must be ever active in God's service. This is what our Lord meant when He said: "If any man will come after me [that is, on the road to heaven, which has to pass through Calvary], let him deny himself, and take up his cross daily, and follow me" (Lk 9:23). Living the Christian religion does not exclude other occupations which are of themselves worldly, but it means these other occupations must be carried out in a true Christian spirit.

As God in His wisdom keeps the hour of our death hidden from us, and as our eternity will depend on the state of our soul at the moment the call comes, the only rational resolution a sane man can make is that he will strive to be ready whenever and wherever the call may come. The following three parables will help us obey God's roadsigns on our earthly journey.

THE VIGILANT SERVANTS

"Let your loins be girt, and lamps burning in your hands. And you yourselves like to men who wait for their lord, when he shall return from the wedding; that when he cometh and knocketh, they may open to him immediately. Blessed are those servants, whom the Lord when He cometh, shall find watching. Amen I say to you, that He will gird himself, and make them sit down to meat, and passing will minister unto them. And if he shall come in the second watch, or come in the third watch, and find them so, blessed are those servants" (Lk 12:35–38).

EXPLANATION: In the parable of the rich fool (p. 36) our Lord taught us how utterly foolish is the man who devotes all his time and energies to acquiring the goods of this world, and makes no provision for eternal life. According to St. Luke's Gospel the Savior then went on to urge His followers to beware of any such folly: "Therefore I say to you, be not solicitous for your life, what you shall eat; nor for your body, what you shall put on. The life is more than the meat, and the body is more than the raiment . . ." (Lk 12:22–23.)

Then He adds three parables inculcating the necessity of vigilance on the part of all, lest the hour of judgment should find them unprepared. As the first two of these parables have the same lesson to teach, we shall treat them as one, and deduce one application from both.

The simile used by our Lord in the first parable was drawn from everyday life in Palestine at that time. When the householder went out at night, he expected his servants to wait up and be ready for his first knock. Doors were not locked by latch and opened with a key at the time, neither were there electric switches; and so if the master was not to be kept waiting on the doorstep, the servants should be on the alert to withdraw the large wooden bolt from the door and to shed the light of their lamps on the entrance the moment he arrived.

Let your loins be girt: The outer dress worn by men and women in the time of our Lord, and even in our day by the Arabs in Palestine, was a long loose robe reaching to the ground. This robe was hitched up and tied around the waist with a girdle when the wearer wished to work or to go on a journey; otherwise the long garment would be a hindrance. When within the house, the girdle was laid aside. This was an indication that one was relaxing and not engaged in any occupation. So the meaning of the command here is: "Be ready for action."

Lamps burning: Night light in those days was provided by lamps. These were small, saucerlike vessels filled with vegetable oil, on which a wick made of a little strip of cloth floated. When lighted, this wick gave forth a tiny uncertain flame as well as much malodorous smoke. A well-to-do household would have many such lamps, and they demanded frequent attention.

And you yourselves like to men who wait for their lord: The picture here is that of a household of servants who are to be in readiness to welcome their master at whatever moment he returns.

When he shall return from the wedding: The master is depicted as being absent at a wedding festival of some friend or relative. These festivals usually dragged on late into the night or early morning hours, and no invited guest could tell beforehand when he could expect to return home. The servants therefore must be ready all night.

Blessed are those servants, whom the Lord when he cometh, shall find watching: The well-prepared servants will receive their master's thanks and praise, nay more:

He will gird himself and . . . minister unto them: Instead of asking them to serve him, he will get them to recline at table and will become their servant, so great will be his gratitude.

Such proof of good pleasure would hardly be given or expected from any earthly master, but our Lord here intermingles the higher lesson with its earthly counterpart. The Lord of heaven will treat His servants whom He finds ready when He comes to call them in this manner: He will get them to recline at the heavenly banquet and He will be their host and eternal Benefactor.

And if he shall come in the second watch, or come in the third watch: The uncertainty of the hour of his coming is stressed, but the servant who is ever ready will not be found "sleeping" (Mk 13:36), and happy will be his lot. The Roman system of dividing the night into four watches of three hours each was in use in Palestine at the time of Christ. St. Mark mentions each of the four watches as the possible time of arrival of the master; St. Luke mentions only the second and third — that is, any time between 9 p.m. and 3 a.m. These watches were the most difficult hours for keeping vigil, and therefore emphasize the vigilance and the merit of the watchful servants.

THE THIEF IN THE NIGHT

"But this know ye, that if the householder did know at what hour the thief would come, he would surely watch, and would not suffer his house to be broken open. Be you then also ready: for at what hour you think not, the Son of Man will come" (Lk 12:39, 40).

EXPLANATION: Our Lord changes the simile. He compares His coming now to that of a thief in the night, a sudden and unexpected arrival.

If the householder did know at what hour the thief would come: Secrecy is the essence of a successful robbery. If the robber announced the time of his intended visit, he would get the reception he deserved. No sane man would go off to sleep if he knew a robber was coming that night.

And would not suffer his house to be broken open: Breaking into a house may suggest much crashing of glass or splintering of wood to our modern minds. It was a much more silent, and easy, operation in Palestine at the time of Christ. Most houses had walls of clay and osier, in which a dagger or sword could easily and silently cut a large hole. Complete wakefulness, then, was necessary in those days if one was to foil a robber.

Be you then also ready; for at what hour you think not, the Son of Man will come: Our Lord applies the parable to His hearers. Just as the householder must be ever on guard if he wishes to preserve his property from robbers, so must the followers of Christ be ready to meet their judge if they wish to avoid being taken unprepared.

At what hour you think not: There will be two comings of our Lord for each of us, the first when we are called to the particular judgment at the moment of death, the second coming will be at the general judgment when Christ will come to judge all mankind. The day and the hour and the year of both are kept hidden from us in God's all-wise providence. It is to his first coming that Christ is referring here, for our sentence in the particular judgment will decide our eternal fate in the second; and besides, there is no purpose in recommending vigilance after death, the time of trial being over. The particular judgment seals the fate of each one. If there are people living on earth when the general judgment comes, their two judgments will be almost simultaneous, but it is each one's particular judgment that will decide his future.

APPLICATION: By giving these repeated warnings to His followers on the necessity of being ready to meet Him when He comes as judge, our Lord proves His divine knowledge of our weak human nature. Christians are men and women who know that this life is only a short period of trial in which they may merit heaven. They know that their eternity begins at their death, that the nature of their eternity will depend on the state of their soul at that moment of death. They also know from the universal experience of the human race that no matter at what age death comes, it is unexpected. Therefore the logical conclusion for the Christian who knows that his eternal happiness depends on his being found "ready" at the moment of death is that he must be always in the state of grace. Yet do the majority act according to this strict logic? Are most Christians ready at any moment to step out of this world and face the judgment on which their eternity will depend? Unfortunately they are not. Many who are prudence itself when it comes to worldly affairs, men who will spend hours deliberating lest they lose a few dollars in a business deal, men who will take every precaution to protect their health, their good name, their position, which can last only a few years at most, frequently act like irresponsible children when it is a question of their eternal destiny.

Nobody is so insane as to deny the fact of death, yet this fact is one which most people strive to keep far from their thoughts. We grow to adult age surrounded by relatives and friends; one by one they drop out of the picture and others take their places. We always find explanations and reasons for their deaths, reasons and explanations which of course do not apply to us — we persuade ourselves that we are immune to all the mortal ills that affect all others. While the fact of death is certain, its time and place are most uncertain, and are beyond our control. But its manner is left for us to decide. The state of our soul at the moment of death will decide our eternal fate.

We may be tempted here to ask why our Lord does not make known the exact day and year of our death, so that we could prepare properly for it. A moment's reflection on the weakness of our human nature will give us the answer. How many of us would resist the temptations to sin which the devil, the world, and the flesh are daily pressing upon us, if we were certain the hour of death was far away and that there was time for repentance? How many would fiulfill their purpose in life which is to know, love, and serve God on earth and thereby merit heaven, if they had foreknowledge of the hour of their death and would therefore wrongly persuade themselves that they could make amends in the few hours before death for a life ill-spent? And, furthermore, what guarantee have we that God would give us the grace of repentance on our deathbeds? Could the human heart and soul that had ignored God for a lifetime turn to him with sincerity and seriousness in the midst of its death throes? Heaven is the reward offered to those who love and serve God during their lives, not during their dying moments, and because the uncertainty of the hour of death is a great help to all of us to keep us faithful, our Lord decreed to keep that hour hidden from us. "Be ready," then, is our Lord's exhortation to all of us, "for you know not the day nor the hour."

But, one may object, is not this asking too much of human nature? How can I be expected to be ever on my knees, ever concentrated on spiritual things; have I not to provide the necessities of life for myself and my dependents? The answer is of course that God does not ask me to be always on my knees, but rather to be up and doing my daily tasks. Our earthly occupations can be compared to stepping-stones which enable us to cross a river; if we use them for their lawful purpose we get across, if we fail to use them we get carried down by the current. Remember the servants in the parable had their tasks to do, and it was in doing them faithfully that they proved they were ready to welcome their master.

It would be wise for all of us to check on ourselves periodically to see if we are so carrying out our earthly occupations that we could at any moment face the Lord's judgment. The good-living Christian who frequents the sacraments regularly and strives honestly to do his duty need have no fear. Our Lord is infinitely merciful; He will be near at the moment of crisis to the follower who always tried to remain close to Him, and the Christian who has been accustomed during his lifetime to calling on God's mercy will not fail to call on it in his moment of danger. But the lukewarm or worldly Christian can hardly expect his religion to play an important role in his last moments — the pangs of death improve very few. And the man who has spent his life apart from God can hardly presume that God will be close to him in his last moments. The time to turn to Him is now; the Master is returning very soon, and for some tomorrow will be too late.

STEWARDS—FAITHFUL AND UNFAITHFUL

"And the Lord said: Who (thinkest thou) is the faithful and wise steward, whom his lord setteth over his family, to give them their measure of wheat in due season? Blessed is that servant, whom when his lord shall come, he shall find so doing. Verily I say to you, he will set him over all that he possesseth. But if that servant shall say in his heart: My lord is long a coming; and shall begin to strike the menservants and maidservants, and to eat and to drink and be drunk: The lord of that servant will come in the day that he hopeth not, and at the hour that he knoweth not; and shall separate him, and shall appoint him his portion with unbelievers" (Lk 12:42–46).

EXPLANATION: The urgent exhortations to watchfulness made by our Lord in the two previous parables must have fallen with startling effects on the ears of His followers. To the Apostles and especially to Peter, so full of honest fervor and so sure of his loyalty to Christ, these reminders seemed inapplicable, just as a few days later in the supper room when the master foretold that all the disciples would be scandalized that night because of him, Peter boldly proclaimed that that would never happen to himself: "Although all shall be scandalized in thee, I will never be scandalized" (Mt 26:33). And so now Peter asks if our Lord's exhortations to watchfulness were intended for the chosen Apostles, or were they rather for those outside the apostolic circle. Christ answers Peter by telling another parable which brings home the truth that the need for vigilance is all the greater the higher one's position of trust.

Who (thinkest thou) is the faithful and wise steward: The simile is taken again from everyday life. In a well-to-do family at that time there were many servants who formed part of the household and who were paid in kind, each receiving board and lôdging as well as a fixed quantity of wheat or other produce of the land which they could dispose of at their will.

Steward . . . over his family [household]: The householder intends to be absent with his family for some indefinite period, and so he appoints one of the servants as master of the household. This steward has the duty to look after his master's interests, and to act toward the other servants as the master himself would.

Blessed is that servant: If the steward carries out his duties faithfully and continues to do so until the master's return, he will earn the praise of the master and will be promoted to be steward for life over all the master's affairs, the highest position a servant could attain.

"But if that servant shall say in his heart: My lord is long a coming: Our Lord now gives the reverse of the medal, the other sad possibility. It could happen that as the master's absence was prolonged the servant who had been given a position of confidence should begin to abuse this position and to use his delegated power to indulge his own evil desires. Power perverts many, as history proves, and even delegated or subordinated power when exercised for a long period is liable to turn the weak man into a tyrannous dictator. This is what our Lord warned against, this is what happened to the promoted servant.

And shall begin to strike the menservants . . . and be drunk: To show his authority he maltreated his fellow servants and gave himself up to riotous living. He usurped the right to deal with his master's subjects and property as he pleased.

The lord of˙that servant will come: The return of the master for such a servant will surely be unexpected and will find him unprepared.

And shall separate him, and shall appoint him his portion with unbelievers: The faithful steward was promoted to the highest position of trust by the master; the unfaithful one will be cast out of the household. The Greek word which we translate by "cast out" literally signifies "cut in two," a punishment frequently meted out to unfaithful slaves in the ancient world. Here in the parable the meaning is that the unfaithful servant of Christ will be excluded from God's kingdom because he failed to live up to the loyalties he professed.

APPLICATION: Our Lord's answer to Peter is clear and unambiguous. God's stewards are appointed and ordained to distribute God's "measure of wheat," His graces, namely, of instruction and sacraments to the members of the household "in due season." Woe to them if they should grow lax in their duty or fail in their task, for thereby they will bring eternal ruin not only on themselves but on countless other souls. And what our Lord said to pastors of souls through Peter is true also of all those who have been placed by God in positions of authority over others here on this earth.

Parents have the God-given duty to set their children on the road to heaven by word and example. Should they fail in this, their life's task is a failure. This is a duty which they cannot delegate to others. Neither the school nor the church can take their place here. The love and knowledge of God must be kindled in the child's heart by the parents and respect for God's law must be fostered by the observance of His commandments in the home. Fathers and mothers, stop for a moment and look into your souls. Have you been acting as the wise and faithful steward whom the master set over his household? Have you given to your children in due season the good example, the timely correction, the Christian instruction which will be their food of life, their training for eternity? Or have you been the unfaithful steward who has been maltreating not only physically, but, what is far worse, morally, the household committed to your care? Have you by your neglect of God and His commandments in the home set your children's feet on the path of destruction? Has your evil example blighted the flowering love of God and His justice in their tender souls? For your sakes and for theirs, God grant that it was not so, but if it were, there may still be time to shut the floodgates of evil that you have opened. Remember that it is not only the future eternal happiness of your own soul and the souls of your children that is at stake, but the souls of their children and their children's children for unknown generations to come.

Teachers also are stewards placed by God over His household. They have the privilege and the duty of directing the youth committed to their care on to the road which leads to life. To fulfill this vocation it is not expected or demanded that each teacher should expound Christian doctrine. But it is expected and demanded by the divine Headmaster that the teacher should instill into his pupils a reverence for God and for His laws through the good example of his conduct in and out of the school. The young are by nature hero worshipers. Their teachers, because of their academic standing and authority, are to be admired and imitated. Grave is the fault, then, and long-lasting the evil consequence, of the bad headline set by a teacher. Truly, in this case, "the evil men do, lives after them." But, thanks be to God, the good teacher's deeds will live after him too, and we are told in Scripture that among those who will shine like stars in heaven will be the teachers who led their pupils on the way of salvation (cf. Dn 12:3).

Other stewards to whom God has given responsibility and authority in His household on earth are civil administrators. Too often, alas, have civil authorities imitated the unfaithful steward, and never more so in the course of history than in our own day. The false materialistic philosophy of the past century has deluded the unthinking and has led to the dethronement of God in many regions. And the new era of freedom promised to the masses turned quickly into the age of bondage. The beneficent bonds of the ten commandments were immediately replaced by the iron shackles of the dictator's whims; the earthly paradises proved to be Siberian salt mines or barbaric extermination camps. Where the state authorities realize that they are stewards of God who have an important and well-defined task to perform, and while they endeavor to carry out their task in all justice and honesty, there cannot and there will not be any conflict between them and the divine authority that God has placed on earth. Such authorities can claim and will always get the loyalty of those who also owe allegiance, and are loyal, to the higher divine power, for it was the divine Master who commanded them to "render to Caesar the things that are Caesar's, and render to God the things that are God's."

WISE AND FOOLISH VIRGINS

"Then shall the kingdom of heaven be like to ten virgins, who taking their lamps went out to meet the bridegroom and the bride. And five of them were foolish, and five wise. But the five foolish, having taken their lamps, did not take oil with them: but the wise took oil in their vessels with the lamps. And the bridegroom tarrying, they all slumbered and slept. And at midnight there was a cry made: Behold the bridegroom cometh, go ye forth to meet him. Then all those virgins arose and trimmed their lamps. And the foolish said to the wise: Give us of your oil, for our lamps are gone out. The wise answered, saying: Lest perhaps there be not enough for us and for you, go ye rather to them that sell, and buy for yourselves. Now whilst they went to buy, the bridegroom came: and they that were ready, went in with him to the marriage, and the door was shut. But at last came also the other virgins, saying: Lord, Lord, open to us. But he answering said: Amen I say to you, I know you not. Watch ye therefore, because you know not the day nor the hour" (Mt 25:1–13).

EXPLANATION: To impress the supreme need of vigilance, our Lord tells another story which shows that some of His followers who have been chosen to play a special role in the nuptials of Christ with His Church, through carelessness and not positive malice, will forfeit their place at the eternal nuptials in heaven.

The image of a marriage to describe Christ's union with His Church was easily understood by His hearers. God's union with the Chosen People of the Old Testament was frequently compared to a marriage, God being the Spouse, Israel the bride (cf. Canticle of Canticles; Is 54; 2 Cor 11:2; Eph 5:25-32).

Then shall the kingdom of heaven be like to ten virgins: "Then" refers to the second coming of Christ in glory, to judge all mankind. On that day His kingdom will be completed; the kingdom on earth, the preparatory period in His Church, will end, and the eternal triumphal kingdom in heaven will begin. The story He now tells illustrates what will happen on that day to some of those He had chosen, and to whom He had given every facility to reach their one and only goal.

Ten virgins: A wedding among the Jews at the time of Christ was preceded by a week of feverish preparations on the part of the bride assisted by her chosen attendants, unmarried maidens of her own age. The wedding feast generally took place in the bridegroom's home. He, accompanied by his companions, "friends of the bridegroom," came to the bride's home about sunset. Having received his bride from her parents or guardians, a procession was formed, and with music and joyful chant the wedding group went to the bridegroom's home, for the wedding feast, which would last all night and perhaps even for days. The invited guests were generally numerous, the relatives and friends of both families, as well as the outstanding people of the neighborhood; and oriental hospitality could not exclude casual acquaintances and strangers should they drop in. The expenses were not as formidable as one might think, for each guest donated flour, cheese, wine, and other useful items, instead of an expensive gift.

In this parable our Lord describes the fate of very special guests, the intimate friends of the bride, who gladly accept the invitation and went to a lot of trouble to prepare for the occasion, and yet, through carelessness, were found unworthy to share in the festivities.

Taking their lamps: The chosen bridesmaids had to carry lighted lamps in the bridal procession, which always took place at night. All ten came to the bride's home in good time, dressed for the occasion and carrying the necessary lamps. These lamps were generally small, shallow earthenware or bronze vessels which held enough oil to burn for a few hours.

And five of them were foolish, and five wise: The number ten was held in high honor among the Jews, and so there were generally ten bridesmaids to accompany a bride on her wedding procession. The folly of the five is shown below.

Having taken their lamps, did not take oil with them: They came to the bride's home early in the day. They remembered to take their lamps but forgot to take a supply of oil with them. This supply was carried in a small vessel or jar when one was going on a journey, as it would be almost impossible to keep the oil from spilling out of the saucerlike lamps. The wise bridesmaids realized they were going as torchbearers in this bridal procession and took a supply of oil for their lamps.

And the bridegroom tarrying: Having gathered in the bride's home, there was much chatter and talk at first; everybody was happy and excited. The foolish as well as the wise looked forward eagerly to the great wedding feast in which they would participate, but as the night wore on they all gradually grew tired until finally they fell into a sound sleep.

Behold, the bridegroom cometh: About midnight a watchman, stationed outside the house to give warning as soon as he saw the bridegroom's party approaching, shouted: "Behold, he comes; get ready to meet him."

Then all those virgins arose and trimmed their lamps: The wise virgins poured in oil and lighted the wicks. The foolish ones just lighted the wick and only when the flame flickered and died did they realize their foolish negligence.

Give us of your oil: Now they try to borrow what they should have provided for themselves.

The wise answered saying: Lest perhaps there be not enough for us and for you, go ye rather to them that sell and buy for yourselves: This answer may sound unkind and uncharitable, but it was only another proof of the wise bridesmaids' prudence.

Whilst they went to buy: For want of any better solution to their problem, the five foolish bridesmaids went out in search of a dealer from whom they could purchase some oil. In the meantime the procession was formed, and went to the bridegroom's home. The door was shut, and the celebration began.

But at last came also the other virgins: After a long search, perhaps in vain at that late hour, they reached the bridegroom's house. Relying on the fact that they were the chosen friends of the bride, the foolish virgins beseeched the bridegroom to let them enter.

But he answering said: Amen I say to you, I know you not: Their claim to admission was not substantiated by the facts. The bride had selected them as her attendants, but they had proved themselves unworthy of this honor; they had not prepared themselves for the privilege offered them. Thus the bridegroom does not acknowledge them.

Watch ye therefore, because you know not the day nor the hour: The conclusion to be drawn from this story by the disciples is this: the time of arrival of our Lord as judge of the universe — the day on which the eternal wedding feast of Christ with His elect will begin — is as uncertain as was the hour of arrival of the bridegroom in the story. There is but one sure way to be found ready on that all-important moment — constant preparedness.

APPLICATION: Although commentators and writers have found difficulty in explaining many of the details in this parable, the general lesson is clear enough. Our Lord described an incident that happened or could have happened at a wedding festival in order to bring home to His listeners the need for being ever vigilant and ready in His service if they wish to avoid the calamity of being excluded from the heavenly and eternal nuptials on the last day. In the other parable in which our Lord uses a wedding feast to describe His kingdom, the lesson concerns those who refused the invitation and will not come to the wedding. Here it concerns those who gladly accepted the invitation.

The ten bridesmaids, or virgins, in the parable represent all Christians. On receiving the sacrament of Baptism, the Christian starts on the road to heaven; he gets his invitation to the heavenly nuptials but this is only the beginning. From the moment he comes to the use of reason he is expected to prepare himself, by living according to the law of God, for the great moment when the call will go forth: "Behold the bridegroom! Come to meet him." This moment will be, first, at the hour of death for each individual when each one's eternal fate will be decided, and again at the general judgment of the whole human race. During their lifetime all are invited to the heavenly wedding, and all have the necessary means to get ready. But, like the foolish bridesmaids, many will fail to make use of these means and will realize their folly when it is too late. Sad, but true.

A certain number of those for whom Christ died on the cross, and to whom He gave the gift of His revelation and offered all the helps they needed, will never reach heaven because they exchanged their heavenly birthright for a mess of earthly pottage. That the foolish bridesmaids in the parable lost a golden opportunity through their negligence is evident and we can all sympathize with them up to a point, but the thoughts of very few will turn to the bride and groom who were so seriously insulted by this act of negligence on the part of chosen friends.

So too, every Christian soul lost is a grievous insult to the God who created and redeemed it. Christians have received the fullness of God's revelation, and have been offered a special place in His marriage festival; they have received a privileged invitation not given to others. Is it not a serious and deliberate insult to God not to comply with the conditions of that generous offer?

Providing themselves with oil was the obligation imposed on the bridesmaids in the parable. It was surely a trivial condition when compared with the reward offered them: a very special place at the marriage feast. The obligations imposed on us Christians are surely trivial too when compared with the reward offered us in return: an eternity of happiness in heaven. It seems incredible that there are many among us this very day who, like the foolish bridesmaids, doze and sleep contentedly holding empty lamps in their hands, while at any moment they may be awakened by: "Behold, the bridegroom comes! Go forth to meet him." It will be too late then to do anything; even their best friends cannot help them. Each one must stand before the judge just as he is; there can be no borrowing of the oil of merit from others and there will be no time to buy any.

Now is the time for all of us to say: "Lord, Lord, open to us," open to us the doors of Your mercy and kindness, and open to us the eyes of our understanding that we may see our defects and remedy them while there is yet time.

It is up to me now to decide, aided by God's grace, where I shall be found on the last day — with the wise bridesmaids or with the foolish.

Infinite Mercy for All

One of the sources of our happiness in heaven will be the contemplation of the mysteries of the divine nature. Our finite, limited intellects can never, even in heaven, fully comprehend all the perfections of God. And wide as our knowledge grows, there will still be some new facet of these mysteries being revealed to us for all eternity. But of all God's mysteries of which we have some knowledge here on earth, the one that astounds us most, and the one on which our future fate depends so completely, is the mystery of His infinite mercy.

The whole Old Testament is one long record of God's merciful dealings with the stubborn and stiff-necked Jews. The New Testament begins with the crowning act of divine mercy for men — the Incarnation — and its pages are filled with outstanding proofs in deed and word of the infinite mercy of the Son of God during His sojourn among us. The following parables are not only convincing proofs of this divine mercy in our regard, but they have been, and they will be for all time, the source of strength and confidence for the hapless sinners who strive to rise from sin and return to their Father's home.

THE LOST SHEEP AND THE LOST COIN.   THE PRODIGAL SON. THE TWO DEBTORS

The following three parables were our Lord's answers to the Scribes and Pharisees who objected to his familiar intercourse with publicans and sinners. In the eyes of the self-righteous Pharisees these two classes of people were the dregs of society. The publicans were Jews appointed by the Romans to collect the imperial taxes from their fellow Jews. In carrying out this task, they frequently sinned against justice, it is true, but their greatest offense was that they aided the pagan foreign usurper, Rome. The sinners, distinct from the publicans, were those Jews who were not overscrupulous in their observance of the numerous major precepts of the Mosaic law, and who ignored or despised the thousands of secondary precepts invented by, and so dear to, the Pharisees. The publicans and sinners were attracted to Christ by His kindness and mercy. They acknowledged their guilt and sought One who could help them mend their ways.

That Christ could deal familiarly with such people went against all the ingrained prejudices of the Scribes and Pharisees. God could not and would not bother with such dregs of humanity. The messianic kingdom was for the respectable and the upright. How could Christ be the Messias if He associated with such people?

The Pharisees had already raised similar objections when Christ allowed the sinful woman to wash and anoint His feet (cf. Lk 7:36–50); and again when He dined in the house of Matthew the publican (cf. 9:9–13). On both occasions Jesus told His critics that His mission was "to call sinners, not the just," for "they that are well have no need of a physician, but they that are sick" (Mk 2:17). He gives them the same answer in the following parables, namely, that His mission is a mission of mercy. We shall treat the parables of the lost sheep and the lost coin together because of the similarity of their main ideas and of their application; the parable of the prodigal son requires separate exposition.

THE LOST SHEEP AND THE LOST COIN

"And he spoke to them this parable, saying: What man of you that hath an hundred sheep: and if he shall lose one of them, doth he not leave the ninety-nine in the desert, and go after that which was lost, until he find it? And when he hath found it, lay it upon his shoulders, rejoicing: And coming home, call together his friends and neighbours, saying to them: Rejoice with me, because I have found my sheep that was lost? I say to you, that even so there shall be joy in heaven upon one sinner that doth penance, more than upon ninety-nine just who need not penance. Or what woman having ten groats; if she lose one groat, doth not light a candle, and sweep the house, and seek diligently until she find it? And when she hath found it, call together her friends and neighbours, saying: Rejoice with me, because I have found the groat which I had lost. So I say to you, there shall be joy before the angels of God upon one sinner doing penance" (Lk 15:3–10.)

EXPLANATION: Palestine was a pastoral country, every village and every district having its shepherds and flocks of sheep and goats. These flocks were the mainstay of the country's economy. Anyone hearing this parable would have acted in exactly the same manner in the given circumstances.

Leave the ninety-nine: This does not mean the ninety-nine other sheep were unprovided for or unprotected. No shepherd will risk losing ninety-nine sheep in order to recover one, but the emphasis is on the extra effort put forth for the sake of the one who strayed.

Lay it upon his shoulders: The shepherd does not make the sheep walk back; he brings it back "rejoicing." The weight is as nothing, because he is so glad to have found the stray.

Calls together his friends and neighbors . . . Rejoice with me: The shepherd's joy is so great that he has to share it with his friends and neighbors, so he calls them to his sheepfold or residence to tell them the good news. The woman in the second parable acts in a like manner. This presupposes a community spirit, a fraternal bond which exists and always existed among the poor and less sophisticated. The fellow shepherds and the woman's neighbors feel the loss of the sheep and the coin almost as if it were their own, and so they rejoice at the finding of the lost property.

I say to you: Our Lord Himself applies the parable so that nobody can mistake His meaning. The shepherd is God; the lost sheep is the sinner; the friends and neighbors are the inhabitants of heaven.

The Divine Shepherd, Christ ("I am the good shepherd" — Jn 10:11) goes out in search of His lost sheep, finds them, and carries them back on His shoulders. This image should have been clear enough to the Pharisees, who read their Scripture. Isaias had foretold seven centuries previously when speaking of the Messias: "Surely he hath borne our infirmities and carried our sorrows . . . he was wounded for our iniquities, he was bruised for our sins: the chastisement of our peace was upon him, and by his bruises we are healed. All we like sheep have gone astray, every one hath turned aside into his own way: and the Lord hath laid on him the iniquity of us all" (Is 53:4–6).

The good shepherd lays down his life for his sheep; Christ laid down His life for us sinners. He carried the Tree of Death on His shoulders to Calvary so that we might have the Tree of Life which Adam forfeited for himself and for us by his disobedience in Eden.

The penitent sinner is welcome, then, in the kingdom of God, and the whole heavenly court rejoices at his repentance.

Upon ninety-nine: The emphasis, as we saw above, is on the lost one — the sinner who returns — not on the others who did not fall away. We must not see any special meaning in the ninety-nine or in the detail that only one of the hundred got lost — these numbers are given to make the story vivid. There are many who do not sin, grievously at least, and many who do, but the whole emphasis of the story is on the mercy of God, who goes looking for the lost sheep even though He does not strictly need to do so. The same holds for the lost coin. The housewife could have done without it, as she had nine others, but the place of the coin was with the others. God wants all to be saved, even those who deliberately offend Him.

What woman having ten groats: The drachma was a silver coin, worth about twenty-five cents, in use in Palestine at the time of our Lord. It was customary for a Jewish girl to receive a necklace or string of coins as part of her dowry at her marriage. It is probably to such an ornament that the parable refers. A married woman would like to preserve such a token intact, just as a wife today will zealously guard her wedding ring. By some accident one of these coins falls off, and the housewife is very worried. She lights a lamp, the interior of Palestinian homes being dark even in daylight, for they had no windows usually. She sweeps the floor from wall to wall, and searches diligently until she finds the coin.

Then, like the shepherd, she is so happy she calls in her neighbors to share her joy.

Our Lord adds the same application of the parable as He gave above concerning the lost sheep.

The angels of God: All the citizens of heaven, even the angels, who are higher beings than man, will rejoice over the sinner who repents and is saved. Knowing as we do that the fallen angels, Satan and his followers, are out to do all in their power to prevent us humans from reaching heaven (cf. 1 Pt 5:6), it is consoling for us therefore to know that we have the good angels on our side; they know all that goes on here on earth, and they are interested in our welfare.

APPLICATION: The lesson these parables have for us is clearly a lesson of hope and confidence in the great mercy of God. Are we not all sinners? Have we not all "gone astray" some time or other, and are we not capable of going astray again any moment? Had we only the justice of God to deal with, we might well despair. But in the whole history of God's relations with man we see that His justice is always tempered with mercy. This mercy was apparent in the Garden of Eden; He could have cast Adam and his followers out forever — He did not need them. But He gave them a second chance by promising to send a Redeemer. They could still reach the eternal Eden even though they had lost the earthly one. He did not strike Cain dead when he murdered Abel; rather He forbade anyone to take revenge on him. He gave him a chance to repent. He saved Noah and his family when the world had become so wicked that He had to send the deluge; and He gave timely warning (120 years) to the sinners to amend their ways. Again and again He intervened to save the Jews when their wickedness had brought vengeance upon them.

But the climax and crowning act of God's mercy was the Incarnation, the coming of His only-begotten Son, in human nature, to live on earth, to teach us God's love and mercy and to die for us on the cross in order to reopen heaven for us and lead us there. He left us His Church to teach us the way to heaven. He gave us the sacraments to aid us on the way, and He deigned to remain with us "all days" by His divine assistance and especially by His real presence in the holy Sacrament of the Eucharist.

Every page of the Bible bears witness to God's mercy. Think back on the sinners He met during His lifetime in Palestine — the robbers, the adulterers, the usurers, the publicans. Even among His chosen twelve, there were James and

John looking for profitable positions in His kingdom (cf Mk 10:37), Peter who denied Him (cf. Mt 26:29), Judas the traitor (cf. Mt 26:50). But never did He utter a harsh word against any of them.

No sinners were ever lost and no sinners ever will be lost because of their sins. Sinners are lost only because they will not turn to their merciful Father to ask His forgiveness. Not a day passes but the kind Father sends out merciful calls to His erring children urging them to return to their Father's household. Today one of those calls is in the very words you are reading. There may be another call for you, there may not. Heed this one, and the other will not be necessary.

Turn to God today with a contrite heart. He will do the rest.

THE PRODIGAL SON

"A certain man had two sons: and the younger of them said to his father: Father, give me the portion of substance that falleth to me. And he divided unto them his substance. And not many days after, the younger son, gathering all together, went abroad into a far country: and there wasted his substance, living riotously. And after he had spent all, there came a mighty famine in that country; and he began to be in want. And he went and cleaved to one of the citizens of that country. And he sent him into his farm to feed swine. And he would fain have filled his belly with the husks the swine did eat; and no man gave unto him. And returning to himself, he said: How many hired servants in my father's house abound with bread, and I here perish with hunger? I will arise, and will go to my father, and say to him: Father, I have sinned against heaven and before thee: I am not worthy to be called thy son: make me as one of thy hired servants. And rising up he came to his father. And when he was yet a great way off, his father saw him, and was moved with compassion, and running to him fell upon his neck, and kissed him. And the son said to him: Father, I have sinned against heaven, and before thee, I am not now worthy to be called thy son. And the Father said to his servants: Bring forth quickly the first robe, and put it on him, and put a ring on his hand, and shoes on his feet: and bring hither the fatted calf and kill it, and let us eat and make merry: because this my son was dead, and is come to life again: was lost, and is found. And they began to be merry. Now his elder son was in the field, and when he came and drew nigh to the house, he heard music and dancing: and he called one of the servants and asked what these things meant. And he said to him: thy brother is come, and thy father hath killed the fatted calf, because he hath received him safe. And he was angry, and would not go in. His father therefore coming out began to entreat him. And he answering said to his father: Behold, for so many years do I serve thee, and I have never transgressed thy commandment, and yet thou hast never given me a kid to make merry with my friends! But as soon as this thy son is come, who hath devoured his substance with harlots, thou hast killed for him the fatted calf. But he said to him: Son, thou art always with me, and all I have is thine. But it was fit that we should make merry and be glad, for this thy brother was dead and is come to life again; he was lost, and is found" (Lk 15:11–32).

EXPLANATION: This beautiful parable was the climax of our Lord's answer to the Scribes and Pharisees, who objected to His association with sinners. In the preceding two parables the sheep and the coin were sorely missed by their owners, but here it is not a dumb animal or a precious souvenir which is lost, but a child who had wilfully left a loving father. His was an act of utter selfishness and utter ingratitude — an act which only the merciful loving heart of a father like the one depicted in this parable could forgive.

Father, give me the portion of substance: According to Jewish law, the younger of two brothers had a right to a third of the father's property at the father's death. The father need not give him this portion during his lifetime, but this was often done when the younger son, with the father's approval, wished to set up his own home. Here there is no such intention, as the sequel shows, and no such approval on the father's part. But the father evidently, convinced of his son's determination to leave home and enjoy unrestricted liberty, grants the ungrateful son's request.

Went abroad . . . and wasted his substance, living riotously: To ensure absolute freedom to do as he wished, this young man not only left his father's home but his country as well. He had his own life and his own money to spend; he wanted nobody, no relative or acquaintance, to interfere with his eagerly sought freedom. In the new country of his choice he evidently found many new

friends who heartily approved of all his wild escapades and helped him squander his limited fortune. They remained his friends while he had the wherewithal to finance their sinful schemes, but his fortune, which appeared to him in the flush of youth to be an immense sum of money, quickly passed through his improvident hands like water through a sieve.

There came a mighty famine . . . and he began to be in want: He now finds himself penniless and friendless in a strange land, and to make matters worse this land is visited with a serious famine. In ordinary times a penniless foreigner has a poor chance of survival in any land, but in time of famine when even money cannot buy the means of sustenance for the local citizens, the lot of the penniless foreigner is surely a desperate one. How desperate things were for this young man the story shows:

He went and cleaved to one of the citizens . . . to feed swine: Only a Jew could grasp the depths of degradation to which he had fallen. Swine were unclean animals according to the Jewish law. Jews were forbidden to eat them or have any contact with them. What more vile or more humiliating employment could the son of a well-to-do Jewish family have been given than the task of swineherd?

And he would fain . . . the husks the swine did eat: Not only is his occupation humiliating, but his remuneration is evidently a starvation wage. His lack of nourishment is so great that he envies the happy lot of the swine; they can fill their bellies with husks and roots, but nobody gives him sufficient food to ease the gnawing pain of his hunger.

Returning to himself: The darkest hour is before the dawn. At last he realizes that it is his own sinful folly that brought him to such straits. He returns to himself; that is, he comes to his senses and examines his position.

How many hired servants: He remembers now the well-to-do home he left. His father has many servants who are well provided for and are happy, while here he, the son of that father, is dying slowly of starvation, a forgotten stranger in a foreign land.

I will arise, and will go to my father: In spite of his sinful past, there is still a modicum of manly honesty left in this poor downtrodden soul. Weaker men in his position, overwhelmed by the misfortunes their sins have brought on them, have taken the coward's path of suicide to end their sorrows. This prodigal admits his guilt and is ready to make any atonement he can for his previous offenses against his father and his God, for in offending the one he knows he has offended the other. He does not even dare to think of being reinstated in his former honorable position of son. He is willing now to accept the lowly position of a servant in his father's house, where by honest labor he can earn his daily bread and can make some atonement to the good father he so thoughtlessly offended in his selfish youth.

And rising up he came to his father: Immediately he puts his resolution into practice. He leaves the foreign country and sets out for home.

When he was yet a great way off, his father saw him: What a touching proof of true paternal love. The good father had long since forgotten the injury his son had done him, but the son he could never forget. The vacant chair at every meal renewed the vacuum in that father's heart. It was not by accident that the father saw him from "a great way off"; day after day that father scanned the distant horizon, hoping and praying that the well-known figure of his errant son would appear over those hills and turn their gloomy shadows into a noon-day brilliance. So when he saw the prodigal, he rushed to meet him, fell upon his neck, and kissed him.

Father, I have sinned against heaven and before thee: The son's repentance is sincere. The father's actions speak volumes. The servants are called to dress the prodigal, who felt he no longer had any claim to be a son of such a good father. The first robe, the best ring, the finest shoes are brought forth, the fatted calf kept for a distinguished visitor is killed, a great feast is prepared, for, to the father's mind, nothing is too good for his returned son. He was dead and has returned to life; he was lost and has been found.

So far the lesson Christ wished to convey in telling this story must have been crystal clear to the Pharisees. The publicans and sinners had been prodigal sons; they had left their father's house and had lowered themselves to the degrading status of swineherds by serving their lower carnal instincts. But the grace of God had touched their hearts; they were repentant and humble, and the all-merciful father was receiving them with open arms. Should not this be an occasion of rejoicing for all God's sons? But it was not, as the complaints of the Scribes and Pharisees prove, and so our Lord continues the parable, describing the reaction of the elder son to the reception given by the father to his prodigal brother, and thus portraying to the Pharisees their own attitude toward the repentant publicans and sinners.

Now his elder son was in the field: While the younger son was squandering his fortune, this elder son had helped his father operate the farm. For this he would deserve every credit if his motives were good. But his character, here portrayed, seems to imply the opposite. Returning from his day's toil in the field, he hears the sound of music and dancing. Instead of being glad that his father had some good reason for rejoicing, he immediately gets suspicious.

He called one of the servants: From the servant he learns the cause of this celebration, and

He was angry, and would not go in: He shows his true colors. His brother's return is no cause for him to rejoice. That his father should give the prodigal such a hearty welcome is a cause of jealousy and envy.

His father therefore coming out began to entreat him: The father's heart is big enough to love both sons. He pleads with the elder son to be bighearted and tolerant like himself, and to join with him in welcoming back the prodigal.

For so many years do I serve thee . . . never transgressed thy commandment: How reminiscent of the boastful prayer of the Pharisee in the temple!

As soon as this thy son is come: Envy and bitterness of soul are evident in these words: "thy son," he says, not "my brother"; such a sinner was not worthy to be his brother. Yet the father counts him worthy to be his son!

Never given me a kid . . . for him the fatted calf: The motive of his labor in his father's household was evidently not solely the desire to please his father; he expected personal rewards. The father's answer: "Son, thou art always with me, all I have is thine," indicates that being with the father and working for his good pleasure should have been sufficient recompense for a faithful son, and he was thus making sure of his inheritance.

But it was fit that we should make merry . . . for this thy brother: The father again stresses the fitness of the present celebration. And he stresses the fact that it was the elder son's duty also to take part and to rejoice: "we should make merry," for "this thy brother was dead and is come to life again; he was lost, and is found."

What the final reaction of the elder son was we are not told. Our Lord left the question open, because the decision was up to the Pharisees. The festival was open to them, the father's love was ready to embrace them too. The messianic kingdom was open to all who were willing to keep its two fundamental commandments — true love of God and true love of neighbor.

APPLICATION: This beautiful story — "the pearl of all parables" as it is justly called — was narrated by Christ to bring home to the minds of men the infinite, immeasurable mercy of God and His true fatherly love for all His children. It was spoken in the first instance to the Scribes and Pharisees who objected to Christ's friendly dealings with sinners. These leaders of the opposition, who prided themselves on their external observance of the law, would have no truck with those who were not like themselves, and quickly condemned Christ for his familiarity with such people. Because their own hearts were narrow and constricted by pride and prejudice, they could not admit that the great big, fatherly heart of God could find room for, and give a sincere welcome to, the errant children whom His grace had brought back to the paternal home. They would not therefore admit that the publicans and sinners, and of course the Gentiles who were not only sinners but sin itself, could be given a place in God's messianic kingdom; and rather than share that kingdom with those they so wrongly despised they chose to stay out of that kingdom and used all their endeavors to crush its founder and its foundations.

Christ, who was God, read their innermost thoughts, and knew the wicked scheme they were planning against Him and His kingdom. Yet being God, His mercy was infinite, and in this very parable He pleads with them to soften their hearts and make room for the prodigal brother therein. The father in the parable *entreats* the elder son to come in and join in the welcome festivities for his lost brother. He does not chide him for his lack of true love of his father. The complete absence of fraternal love will all be forgiven as the crimes of the younger son are forgiven, if only the elder son will come to his senses, as the younger son had done. Many Pharisees were later touched by grace, and did as Christ had asked them in this parable, but the majority remained obdurate in their opposition to "sinners" and to Christ, "the Lover of sinners and the Conqueror of sin."

All of us are portrayed in this story; we are either the elder or the younger son. If we are the elder son, and by the grace of God have managed to stay in our Father's home and have avoided the more serious offenses against His law, let us beware of any temptation to boast of this as if we alone deserved the credit. And let us especially try to have a heart like Christ for the younger brother who is not so fortunate as we were. Such a heart will not only not object to the joyful welcome home God gives the prodigal, but it will do all in its power to get the prodigal to return home. Had the elder brother in the parable true love for his father and for his brother, would he not have gone looking for the lost one? But, no, he stayed comfortably at home "minding his own business." Too many good people today are likewise so busy minding their own business, their own salvation, that they cannot spare a moment for the prodigals who are so much in need of help. How often, unfortunately, does one hear: "He made his bed; let him lie on it," or "Let him stew in his own juice" and similar un-Christian expressions from the mouths of "good" people who think they are loyal children of their heavenly Father. Yet the Father loves these prodigal children, and is yearning for their return; His true, loyal child will do all in his power to save his brother, and thereby bring joy to his heavenly Father. Remember, there is no true loyalty to God in the heart of him who does not truly love his brother.

If, on the other hand, we are the younger sons, how graphically our state is depicted in this parable — that desire for liberty, that urge to shake off restrictions, that longing for false freedom, that claiming of the gifts of body and soul as ours to do with as we please when they are not ours, the squandering of these gifts in a foreign land, i.e., the waste of years of valuable life in pursuits that produce nothing but the bitter fruit of shame and regret.

Gloomy indeed, though true to life, is the picture of God's prodigal sons while estranged from Him; and black indeed their final fate if no helping hand were forthcoming to lift them out of the mire of sin. But, and here is where Christ's portraiture is so consoling, there is a helping hand. The hand of God's unlimited mercy is ever stretching out to lift up His fallen children and lead them home.

Prodigals we may have been, but the paternal home is wide open to receive us back. God's messengers of mercy are continually calling us to stop and think, and consider our perilous position. Why should we be starving in an alien land, envying the swine their good fortune, when the road back lies open before us, and all we have to do is to say: "I will arise and go to my father." The almighty and merciful Father will do the rest.

THE TWO DEBTORS

"And one of the Pharisees desired him to eat with him. And he went into the house of the Pharisee and sat down to meat. And behold a woman that was in the city, a sinner, when she knew that he sat at meat in the Pharisee's house, brought an alabaster box of ointment; and standing behind at his feet, she began to wash his feet with tears, and wiped them with the hairs of her head, and kissed his feet, and anointed them with the ointment. And the Pharisee, who had invited him, seeing it, spoke within himself, saying: This man, if he were a prophet, would know surely who and what manner of woman this is that toucheth him, that she is a sinner. And Jesus answering, said to him: Simon I have somewhat to say to thee. But he said: Master, say it. A certain creditor had two debtors, the one owed five hundred pence, and the other fifty. And whereas they had not wherewith to pay, he forgave them both. Which therefore of the two loveth him most? Simon answering, said: I suppose that he to whom he forgave most. And he said to him: Thou hast judged rightly. And turning to the woman he said unto Simon: Dost thou see this woman? I entered into thy house, thou gavest me no water for my feet; but she with tears hath washed my feet, and with her hairs hath wiped them. Thou gavest me no kiss; but she since she came in, hath not ceased to kiss my feet. My head with oil thou didst not anoint; but she with ointment hath anointed my feet. Wherefore I say to thee: Many sins are forgiven her, because she hath loved much. But to whom less is forgiven, he loveth less. And he said to her: Thy sins are forgiven thee. And they that sat at meat with him began to say within themselves: Who is this that forgiveth sins also? And he said to the woman: Thy faith hath made thee safe, go in peace" (Lk 7:36–50).

EXPLANATION: This incident took place in a town in Galilee during the second year of our Lord's public ministry. He has already been marked by the Pharisees as a friend of publicans and sinners. And therefore, to their way of thinking, He cannot be their Messias. However, as yet their opposition has not turned to violent hatred, and especially outside of Jerusalem many of the Pharisees are still anxious to learn more about Him. Perhaps for this very reason the Pharisee invited our Lord to dine with him. He had many questions he would like to ask, and the privacy of the dining room with only a few select fellow Pharisees present was a suitable place for this. Our Lord accepted the invitation, for He never refused an opportunity of offering His message of repentance to all men, Pharisee as well as publican. Because of the woman's sudden intrusion, however, Simon was prevented from asking his prepared questions. Instead, he was given the answer to a more fundamental question as to the nature and mission of Christ.

A woman that was in the city, a sinner: There are many sins by which a woman as well as a man can and does offend God; but from as far back as human records go, the one and only sin which brands a woman as a public sinner was and still is the sin of unchastity.

When she knew that He sat at meat in the Pharisee's house: This poor sinner had seemingly already heard our Lord's call to repentance; she had come to believe in Him and had turned from her evil ways. She now has an opportunity of showing her gratitude to her benefactor, so she bravely faces the stares of the assembled Pharisees in order to prove to her Master that she loves Him and is sincerely grateful to Him for all He has done for her.

Alabaster box of ointment: Her purpose was to anoint the feet of Jesus with this most precious possession she had, a jar of perfumed myrrh. The well-to-do used such an ointment on special occasions for anointing the head, to add luster and perfume to the hair; but to use it on the feet would be considered extravagant waste (cf. Jn 12:5).

She began to wash his feet, with tears: As the oriental custom of dining was to recline on cushions with the head toward a low central table on which the dishes were placed, it was not difficult for the woman to reach Jesus' feet. Having reached them, she was so overcome with repentance for her past misdeeds that she bathed His feet with her tears, and, not having a towel, she did not hesitate to use her long, beautiful tresses which in the past had been part of her sinful allure, to dry those sacred feet. Then kissing them with loving devotedness, she spread the precious ointment over His feet.

And the Pharisee . . . seeing it: What a shock this scene must have been for the host and his fellow Pharisees! They who used to gather their robes tightly about them when walking through the streets lest even their garments should accidentally touch a sinner, have witnessed a woman of ill-repute not only touching but also washing with her tears and repeatedly kissing the feet of One who claims to be holy. He pretends to be the expected Messias, and yet He does not know who and what this woman is — or worse still, if He knows, He allows this dreadful sinner to be so familiar with Him.

Simon, I have somewhat to say to thee: Simon and his fellow Pharisees were not openly critical, but our Lord shows them He has read their secret thoughts, a fact which of itself should prove to them that He is more than a prophet; and He now goes on to show them how wrong their secret criticisms are.

A certain creditor had two debtors: Under the clothing of a parable with its application, our Lord gives the true explanation of the scene they had witnessed, and so defends both His own and the woman's actions in that scene. At the same time He gently reprimands Simon for his lack of courtesy when Christ appeared at his home. The speck of dust Simon had seen in the woman's eye was not there, but there was a beam in his own (cf. Mt 7:1–5).

One owed five hundred pence, the other fifty: The denarius was the daily wage of a laborer. The emphasis here is not so much on the amount owed as on the contrast between the two amounts. One owed ten times more than the other.

Whereas they had not wherewith to pay: For each of the debtors, his debt was a heavy one, for an unpayable debt is a lifelong burden to any honest man. But the creditor was merciful; seeing they could not settle their accounts now nor in the future, he generously remitted their debts. Our Lord then asked Simon which of the debtors will love the creditor the more. And Simon answers correctly — the one to whom the greater debt was remitted.

And turning to the woman, he said: Jesus now goes on to apply the parable to the present circumstances. He contrasts the woman's actions with Simon's. Jesus had come as a guest to Simon's house. It was customary to wash the feet of distinguished guests, to give them the kiss of welcome, and to anoint their head with oil. Simon had done none of these things for Jesus, because he did not look on Him as a distinguished guest, much less the Messias. This good woman, on the other hand, had washed His feet, not with water, but with the hot tears of gratitude — "the blood of her soul," as St. Augustine says — she had covered the feet of our Lord with innumerable loving kisses, and had anointed those same feet, not with ordinary oil, but with the most expensive myrrh she could find.

Wherefore I say to thee: Our Lord now draws the conclusion for Simon which follows from the parable He had proposed above; namely, this woman is no longer what you think she is, a notorious sinner. Her sins have been blotted out. Because she realizes the immensity of the debt which I, her creditor, have remitted to her, she has given these heartfelt demonstrations of great love.*

But to whom less is forgiven, he loveth less: Simon, on the other hand, was, at least in his own estimation, the debtor who owed only a small sum, if indeed he would admit to any indebtedness to God caused by personal sin. As for seeing in Christ the creditor who could remit all debt of sin, as the penitent woman had done, such a thought was far from Simon's mind as it was far

---

* The interpretation of this gospel scene and parable, especially of verse 37, given here is not that commonly given by Catholic authors who see in the acts of the penitent the *cause* of the forgiveness of her sins rather than the *effects* of that forgiveness. But the parable and the whole context seem to demand the interpretation given above, namely, that her great acts of love were a proof of the great debt of sin remitted to her; see P. D. Buzy, S.C.J., *Les Parables* (Verbum Salutis*, VI) (Paris: Beauchesne et Fils, 1948), 6th ed., pp. 238–267. Also Max Zerwick, S.J., *Analysis Philologica N.T. Graeci* (Rome, 1953), p. 153.

from the minds of all his fellow Pharisees. And so, as Jesus pointed out, Simon did not consider himself deeply in debt to God, and in no way whatsoever in debt to Jesus. Hence the contrast between his cold reception of our Lord and the overflowing gratitude and love of the penitent who knew and admitted she had so much for which she ought to be grateful.

Thy sins are forgiven thee: These words of Christ are not the words of absolution, but a public declaration of what has already taken place. Our Lord had already declared in a preceding verse that her sins had been forgiven. This statement of Christ was a supreme consolation to the penitent, but it was also a proof to Simon that Christ was not only a prophet, which Simon had doubted, but someone much greater; for He knows the innermost soul of the penitent, and declares she is free from sin. But what is more, He has taught in the parable that He has remitted her great debt.

And they that sat at meat with him began to say within themselves: This was not lost on the Pharisees; they saw clearly that He was claiming to be the one who had forgiven this penitent, but "God alone can forgive sins." "Who is this that forgiveth sins also?" they asked; in other words, is he not claiming to be God? He was, and He meant them to realize this.

Thy faith hath made thee safe, go in peace: Once more He shows how superior to the Pharisees is this sinner they so despise. She has believed that Christ is the Messias who has come to take away "the sin of the world" (Jn 1:29). She has believed that He had the mercy and the power to remove her personal sins, great as they were, provided she truly repented. She has repented, she has been forgiven everything, and Christ now tells her to go in peace — in peace with God and with her own conscience.

APPLICATION: In the parables of the lost sheep and the prodigal son, our Lord has shown us how God, the loving Father, welcomes back the erring children who return to Him through repentance. But in this gospel incident we have a real description, not a made-up story, of the same merciful loving Shepherd and Father who has come from heaven to bring back all the lost sheep and all the prodigals of the human race. The Saviour's message of hope and encouragement touched the sinner's heart; she looked on the Lover of sinners, and she abandoned forever all sinful love. She who had been the despair of her parents and a scandal to her fellow citizens has become a shining example of repentance to all the sinners of the world, and an abiding proof of the power of divine mercy.

And who is there among us who does not need this example, this encouragement? Our Lord is willing and able to raise up even the most debased and inveterate sinners, if only they will listen to His loving call. In one of the very first sermons of His public ministry, He declared that His mission was one of mercy to those in need. He quoted the prophecy of Isaias concerning the long-awaited Messias: "The spirit of the Lord is upon me, wherefore has He anointed me; to bring good news to the poor. He has sent me, to proclaim to the captives release, and sight to the blind. To set at liberty the oppressed." Only God could so describe the infinite divine mercy; what mere man could dare to expect such limitless compassion and understanding from the Supreme Being? He came to bring the good news of the Gospel to those poor in spiritual possessions, and poor the whole world was until His coming. He came to set the slaves of Satan and of sin free from their cruel bondage, and to give back to men once more the insight to see themselves in their true relationship with God, with their neighbors, and with the world.

And lest anyone should, through false humility, esteem himself unworthy of this divine condescension, and incapable of benefiting by this infinite compassion and mercy, Christ brings in the examples of the bruised reed and the smoking wick. Could anything be more useless and less worthy of attention than a broken reed? Yet He says He has not come to crush and annihilate it, but to give it back its original beauty. Also, the smoking wick is not only useless but offensive to the senses. But even with such a despicable object the divine Redeemer will not act harshly; He will cleanse that wick, relight it, and thereby give purpose to its existence. These were but similes to express the truth that there is no soul so damaged or so disfigured by the ravages of sin that He cannot and will not repair it. Such a soul can become once more an object worthy of the admiration not only of mankind and of the angels but of God Himself.

What a consolation for all of us sin-stained travelers through this valley of tears! In our moments of honest self-examination most of us can see ourselves as bruised reeds and smoking wicks. But we have a God in heaven whose mercy is as infinite as His power; a Father who so loved us that He sent His divine Son on earth to raise up, cleanse, and revivify His human sons and daughters who have made themselves unworthy of that name. And our divine Brother not only taught us the immensity of the divine mercy for man by word and by deed during His earthly sojourn among us, but He set up a society, His Church, which has the authority and the supernatural means to continue His mission of mercy on earth until the end of time. And what does He demand of us in return? That we simply and honestly realize our weaknesses, admit our faults, and humbly implore His merciful forgiveness. The true Christian who has experienced and appreciated the soothing balm of God's merciful forgiveness will never be short of ways in which to return love for love; he will find within easy reach the means, as God's instrument, through which divine love and mercy will reach a brother in need.

S E C T I O N   S E V E N

The Hallmark of Christianity

The incarnation is an act of charity so infinitely great and so far beyond our human comprehension that there are men who deny it ever took place. But thanks to God's infinite love, His Son did become man to atone for the world's sins. He reopened heaven for us on Calvary, and showed us the way and gave us the means to get there. As love — infinite, divine love — was the motive power behind the great mystery of our redemption, it is to be expected that love — human and limited though it be — should be the hallmark of the "redeemed." This is St. John's logical deduction: "If God hath so loved us; we also ought to love one another" (1 Jn 4:11). And here the beloved disciple is but reechoing his Master, who emphatically declared that His true followers should be recognized by their fraternal charity: "A new commandment I give unto you: That you love one another, as I have loved you, that you also love one another. By this shall all men know that you are my disciples, if you have love one for another" (Jn 13:34–35).

Fraternal charity, then, for all are redeemed by Christ, should be the outstanding characteristic of every follower of Christ. Even the lukewarm Christian will admit this in theory, but it takes the arduous efforts of the fervent to put this theory into daily practice. Human nature is selfish, revengeful, unforgiving, blinded by petty prejudices; the true Christian must overcome these evil tendencies if he is to see in all men, at all times, fellow children of God and fellow brothers in Christ. Our merciful Lord knew full well how difficult the practice of this essential Christian virtue would be for us, and therefore He not only gave us the command to love one another, but He showed us in the following practical parables how we ought to overcome selfishness, hardheartedness, prejudice — the archenemies of true Christian charity.

UNSELFISH GENEROSITY

"And he said to him also that had invited him: When thou makest a dinner or a supper, call not thy friends nor thy brethren, nor thy kinsmen, nor thy neighbours who are rich; lest perhaps they also invite thee again, and a recompense be made to thee. But when thou makest a feast, call the poor, the maimed, the lame, and the blind; and thou shalt be blessed, because they have not wherewith to make thee recompense: for recompense shall be made thee at the resurrection of the just" (Lk 14:12–14).

EXPLANATION: Although the Evangelist does not expressly call the above instruction a parable, he inserts it among a series of parables spoken on the same occasion, and it has all the characteristics of a parable. It was given by our Lord to the Pharisee who had invited Him to a meal in order to embarrass Him.*

When thou makest a dinner or a supper: The inviting of others to a meal as a gesture of goodwill and friendship is almost as old as the human race. But unfortunately, what should be an act of pure benevolence has too often been vitiated by self-interest and a not very hidden desire for receiving a similar or equivalent earthly benefit in return. And therefore our Lord said to the Pharisee:

Call not thy neighbours who are rich: The guests among which our Lord found Himself were evidently friends, kinsmen, and wealthy neighbors of the host. Under the guise of an act of benevolence, it was rather the sound investment of a little capital. The guests were chosen because all were capable and likely to do a similar good turn or a better one for their so-called benefactor. It was not so much from benevolence the host acted as from a sound practical sense of business.

Call the poor: Invite those who are

in need, and from whom you cannot expect a recompense. This would be the act of a truly benevolent man who was ready to help his neighbor without any thought of self-interest.

And thou shalt be blessed: Such an action would be truly charitable, and would therefore merit God's blessings and reward.

They have not wherewith to make thee recompense: He who helps the truly needy does so out of a motive other than self-interest, for he cannot expect a recompense from those who have nothing.

At the resurrection of the just: Each one will be justly rewarded or punished at the particular judgment, but at the general resurrection each one will have his definite final reward or punishment, because it is only then that the final results of our actions will have been produced. The good works, and unfortunately the bad works also, which I perform in this century, will keep on producing effects right down to the end of time. God, to whom all things are present, will pass a just sentence at the moment of my death, but it is only at the general judgment that the final balance sheet of my life will be made manifest to the world.

---

* See "The Last Place at a Feast," p. 85.

APPLICATION: Although our Lord mentions only charitable hospitality in the parable, having taken His cue from present circumstances, His lesson was intended to cover the whole field of fraternal charity. The Pharisee who had invited our Lord had evidently expected a goodly return from his guests, while at the same time he was posing as a man who generously shared his earthly goods with his neighbors. But this self-interest and this expectation of earthly recompense turned what could be an act of generous hospitality into a mere act of worldly, prudent investment, and therefore ceased to be charitable and was of no supernatural value. Self-interest, unfortunately, is as universal as human nature, and our Lord's words of warning are as applicable in this twentieth century as they were in the first. Human nature has a deep streak of egoism embedded in it, and this egoism or selfishness keeps bobbing up in the most embarrassing way, especially when we feel called on to give of our time or our goods to a fellow man in need.

The charity which our Lord asked His followers to practice cuts at the very roots of man's innate egoism. Selfishness or self-interest has no place in His commandment. We are called on to help our neighbor because he is a fellow child of God; and not only must we exclude all desire of any earthly gain from that helping hand, but we must be ready at times to help others even at a great personal loss. This is not easy. When it is a question of public subscriptions or of some act that demands a sacrifice but will put us in the headlines, we have the recompense of public recognition; and when we come to the aid of one who may later be in a position to help us, we feel we are making a safe investment. But when true charity calls on us to make a sacrifice for no other motive but that the needy neighbor is a child of God, and that sacrifice will remain a secret between God and ourselves, then our self-loving and self-interested "ego" will offer a hundred excuses to prevent us from acting.

"Charity begins at home" is one of the stock arguments used by our selfish ego. But are you really looking after yourself if you are placing your eternal fate in jeopardy for the sake of a few years of earthly comfort here below? You may have earned every dollar you possess by the sweat of your brow, and you think you have the right to enjoy every cent of it now, but who gave you the bodily strength and health to work? who gave you the grace to keep on the straight and narrow when so many of your acquaintances fell by the way? Has He who invested so much in you any right to a small dividend? But that needy neighbor, the ego continues, has only himself to blame, his misfortunes are the just reward of his own folly. Our hospital wards are full of accident cases resulting from folly and carelessness; have they no right to treatment? or should they be left to die untended? If the good God can find ways of excusing and healing the sinful carelessness and folly of one of His creatures, who am I to condemn that creature? If God is ready to lift him up after his fall, and calls on me to give a helping hand, am I not questioning God's wisdom if I refuse? The cause of life's accidents is not the concern of the doctor, or the true Christian. Only the selfish ego, looking for an excuse for shirking duty, probes the causes.

Another sound practical excuse which our ego offers for not helping a needy neighbor is the maxim: "I mind my own business, and it is a full-time occupation." This is an excellent maxim when applied to purely worldly affairs and actions, and this world would be perhaps a happier place to live in if it were followed by all of us. Meddlers can cause a lot of unnecessary suffering. But does this maxim apply to the supernatural life of God's children on earth? Are we each a separate entity completely insulated from and independent of all others on our journey to heaven? Is not the contrary Christ's teaching? We form the Mystical Body of Christ on earth; He is the head, we are the members. Just as in the physical body, each member of the Mystical Body is intimately and inextricably connected with every other member, and dependent on these other members for his own spiritual health and progress. And so it follows that the spiritual help of one member is the concern of all the other members.

Of course, God does not demand the impossible. I cannot give direct aid to all the ailing members of Christ's Mystical Body; but there is a certain number of these members within my reach whom I can help, and whom God expects me to help. I can and must help all God's children by my prayers. I shall say the prayer after Mass: "Hear our prayers for the conversion of sinners, and for the liberty and exaltation of our holy mother the Church" with deep devotion, for the needs of the whole Mystical Body are included here. Other particular cases or causes which I can help with material aid will be brought to my notice periodically by my pastor or by others. But in my own neighborhood there will be some whom God has allotted to me as my special field of practical unselfish charity. It will not always be material aid that is needed. A word of advice, of encouragement, of consolation, offered at the right moment, an invitation to a lecture, a retreat, or a meeting, the loan or gift of a spiritual book or pamphlet, these and a hundred other ways the charitable soul will find to help a brother in need. It is not what is done, but the motive of true love behind it that matters.

Charity does, after all, begin at home, for the whole world is one big home, and I am minding my own business in the true and highest sense of that phrase when I take a truly charitable and practical interest in the spiritual welfare of my neighbor.

THE MERCILESS SERVANT

"Therefore is the kingdom of heaven likened to a king, who would take an account of his servants. And when he had begun to take the account, one was brought to him, that owed him ten thousand talents. And as he had not where-with to pay it, his lord commanded that he should be sold, and his wife and chil-dren and all that he had, and payment to be made. But that servant falling down, besought him, saying: Have patience with me, and I will pay thee all. And the lord of that servant being moved with pity, let him go and forgave him the debt. But when that servant was gone out, he found one of his fellow servants, that owed him an hundred pence: and laying hold of him, he throttled him, saying: Pay what thou owest. And his fellow servant falling down, besought him, saying: Have patience with me, and I will pay thee all. And he would not: but went and cast him into prison, till he paid the debt. Now his fellow servants seeing what was done, were very much grieved, and they came and told their lord all that was done. Then his lord called him: and said to him: Thou wicked servant, I forgave thee all the debt, because thou besoughtest me: shouldst not thou then have had compassion also on thy fellow servant even as I had compassion on thee? And his lord being angry, delivered him to the torturers until he paid all the debt. So also shall my heavenly Father do to you, if you forgive not every one his brother from your hearts" (Mt 18:23–35).

EXPLANATION: In this parable our Lord teaches us how necessary it is to be merciful to our fellow men if we hope to obtain mercy from God. Jesus had told Peter that he must be ready to forgive an offending brother not only seven times but seventy times seven, that is, times without number, always. This story showed Peter why.

The kingdom of heaven: God's king-dom on earth, the Church.

One was brought . . . owed ten thou-sand talents: This was a huge sum (over six million dollars), which no servant could owe to a king, but the details of a parable are often highlighted to bring out the truth of the lesson. The lesson here is the immense unpayable debt a sinner owes God's justice for even one mortal sin.

His lord commanded that he should be sold: It was the legal practice in many places at the time of Christ to sell into slavery an insolvent debtor and his whole family. The master who bought them would pay the creditor so much per year, the debtor and family remaining in slavery until the whole debt was paid.

That servant falling down, besought him: The servant knew that his only hope for himself and his family was to appeal to his king for mercy. He prom-ised to pay all, which was hardly possible considering the huge debt he owed, but he meant he would keep reducing the debt the rest of his life.

Moved with pity . . . forgave him the debt: The king was generous; he real-ized what a life slavery would be for the servant and family, and so he forgave the debt and set him free. He granted more than was asked of him.

But when that servant was gone out: Now we come to the second scene. On his way out of the courtroom the servant meets a fellow servant who owes him a small sum, a hundred denarii, equal to about ten dollars.

And laying hold of him, he throttled him: The first servant immediately re-sorts to violence.

Pay what thou owest: The sum is so

paltry when compared with the immense debt that had been remitted to himself that most likely he is ashamed to mention the sum — all he says is: "Whatever you owe me."

And his fellow servant falling down besought him: Exactly as he himself had done a few moments before, the second servant now asks for mercy and promises to pay all. This promise was easily fulfilled, whereas the first servant's promise to pay all was not, but there was no mercy or generosity in the first servant's heart.

But went and cast him into prison, till . . . debt: He sees that justice is carried out, that the defaulter is punished.

Now his fellow servants seeing what was done: The third scene. The fellow servants of the two, seeing the meanness and lack of generosity of a man who had just been treated so generously and so mercifully, were much grieved, and they reported the occurrence to their king.

Wicked servant: The fourth and last scene. The first servant is summoned before the king once more, but this time it is not a merciful master he faces but a just judge.

I forgave thee . . . shouldst not thou

then have had compassion: The accusation this time is not that he owed a big debt to the king, but that he has acted unmercifully toward his fellow servant. He had not done to others what he had wished to be done to himself.

And his lord . . . delivered him to the torturers: The master will now demand strict justice. As the debt he owed was immense, it follows that slavery was for life and, what was worse, torture was added to the slavery because of the want of mercy he had shown to his fellow man.

So also shall my heavenly Father: Our Lord now applies the parable. It was a story invented to describe the necessity of practicing mercy toward our neighbor if we wish to obtain mercy from God. In other words, it was an application of that petition in the Lord's Prayer: "forgive us our trespasses as we forgive those who trespass against us." And as our Lord then said: (Mt 6:15) "If you will not forgive men, neither will your Father forgive you your offences" (Mt 6:15). He repeats the same warning here: "so also shall my heavenly Father do to you, if you forgive not every one his brother from your hearts."

APPLICATION: Reading the story of the merciless servant, our natural reaction is to judge him a mean, low type of man, who puts himself outside the pale of mercy. He throttled his fellow man for a paltry ten dollars, and would not listen to the poor man's pleas for mercy. When we hear what the king did to him, we heartily approve and say: "It served him right; he got what he richly deserved." But hadn't we better stop a moment today and reflect that we ourselves may be that merciless servant? Every time we have sinned mortally we have incurred an unpayable debt to God. Each time we have received absolution from God's representative we have come out of that courtroom free men. A weight greater than a million-dollar debt has been lifted from our shoulders. A fate worse than generations of earthly bondage — eternal slavery namely — has been spared us because of God's infinite mercy. How then can we be so mean, so ungrateful, and so foolish as to refuse to pardon a neighbor a paltry debt and thus risk reincurring our own huge debt as the merciless servant did? I follow in the footsteps of the merciless servant every time I refuse to forgive my fellow men. He received from the king what he justly deserved; so shall I too if I continue to imitate him.

THE GOOD SAMARITAN

"A certain man went down from Jerusalem to Jericho, and fell among robbers, who also stripped him, and having wounded him went away, leaving him half dead. And it chanced, that a certain priest went down the same way: and seeing him, passed by. In like manner also a Levite, when he was near the place and saw him, passed by. But a certain Samaritan being on his journey, came near him; and seeing him, was moved with compassion. And going up to him, bound up his wounds, pouring in oil and wine: and setting him upon his own beast, brought him to an inn, and took care of him. And the next day he took out two pence, and gave to the host, and said: Take care of him; and whatsoever thou shalt spend over and above, I, at my return, will repay thee. Which of these three, in thy opinion, was neighbor to him that fell among the robbers? But he said: He that shewed mercy to him. And Jesus said to him: Go, and do thou in like manner" (Lk 10:30–37).

St. Luke gives us the setting for this parable: "And behold a certain lawyer stood up, tempting him [Jesus], and saying, Master, what must I do to possess eternal life? But he said to him: What is written in the law? how readest thou? He answering, said: Thou shalt love the Lord thy God with thy whole heart, and with thy whole soul, and with all thy strength, and with all thy mind: and thy neighbor as thyself. And he said to him: Thou hast answered rightly: this do, and thou shalt live. But he willing to justify himself, said to Jesus: And who is my neighbour?" (10:25–29.) In other words, "It's all very fine to say, love your neighbor, but who is he exactly?" According to the common opinion and practice among the Jews, their neighbor was a fellow Jew and no one else; according to some rabbis, non-Jews could be included. Jesus' answer to the question "Who is my neighbour?" is a parable which illustrates who is a real neighbor.

EXPLANATION: The incident our Lord describes here to bring out the lesson on charity is one that must have happened many times. To "fall among robbers" on the lonely road between Jerusalem and Jericho has been the unfortunate lot of many even in our own day. The only building one sees on the way after Bethphage, a few miles outside Jerusalem, is a police station built, it is said, on the site of the inn to which the Good Samaritan carried the injured man. Many wounded and robbed natives and tourists are still carried there.

A priest . . . a Levite: Priests and Levites were the officials of the Temple of Jerusalem. They especially were expected to carry out the commandment of love of neighbor, and help a fellow man in distress. The robbed and injured man was most probably a Jew, for he was a native of Jerusalem, and therefore they could not excuse themselves on the plea that he was not a neighbor even in their restricted sense of the word.

A certain Samaritan: To bring out the contrast all the more, a Samaritan fulfills the law of charity when the priest and Levite had failed miserably to do so. The Samaritans were the inhabitants of Samaria, a mixture of pagan colonists, sent over from Assyria when the kingdom of Israel (northern part of Palestine) was overrun by the Assyrians in 722 B.C., and of the few Jews who were left behind when the prisoners of war were taken away. They developed a new half-pagan, half-Jewish religion, keeping the Pentateuch (the first five books of the Old Testament), hoping for a Messias, but maintaining their own temple on Mount Garizim near Samaria. They were hated by the Jews, who would not so much as bid them the time of day (cf. Jn 4). It was one of these despised half pagans who took compassion on the poor injured Jew, gave him first aid on the roadside, brought him to the inn, stayed the night to look after him, and the next morning offered to pay the Jewish innkeeper for whatever other expense the patient might incur.

Which of these three: Our Lord now applies the parable for the lawyer. The Samaritan had true love of neighbor, and he did not quibble over who his neighbor was. The lawyer is honest enough to admit the truth of this, and so our Lord tells him to "Go, and do thou in like manner."

APPLICATION: Christ Himself is surely the chief Good Samaritan, who binds the wounds and pours the oil of consolation into troubled souls, and has appointed His Church to be the innkeeper who is charged to look after all His afflicted ones until He comes again.

But not only did He set us an example of charity, He has given us a strict command to love one another as He loved us; and He tells us that our sentence on the day of judgment will depend principally on how we fulfilled this special commandment (cf. Mt 25:31–46). It would be well for me today to examine my conscience to see if I am usually a good Samaritan to my needy neighbor. I need not travel on the lonely road from Jerusalem to Jericho to find a neighbor lying by the wayside, the victim of this world's wickedness. But, like the priest and the Levite, do I pass quickly lest my conscience should annoy me? Of course, I have many and good reasons for shirking the responsibility. The priest and Levite had good reasons, too; they did not pass by out of sheer malice; but, strangely enough, our Lord did not mention their excuses.

"Lord, when did we see thee hungry, or thirsty, or a stranger, or naked. . . ?" was the only self-defense the condemned could put up at the judgment (cf. Mt 25:44). There are many self-satisfied "good" Christians who can feel deep compunction on Good Friday, while listening to a sermon on the Passion of our Lord, and who would have done all in their power to relieve His pain had they been on Calvary, they say; but our Lord gives the test of their sincerity Himself:

"Amen I say to you, as long as you did it not to one of these least, neither did you do it to me" (Mt 25:45). His "least" ones, His hungry, His thirsty, His naked, are all around you, all within easy reach of any sincere Christian today. It is not the amount you give or the time you devote to the help and the care and comforting of the afflicted; it is the sacrifice you make out of your own meager funds and out of your busy day that will be reckoned to you as a charitable act well done. Even the poorest and the busiest cannot be excused from the corporal works of mercy; they are binding on all.

If helping a neighbor over a material hurdle is an obligation on all, how much greater is our obligation to help them over the spiritual hurdles of life? Here, too, there are many of our fellow men, our neighbors, lying wounded by the wayside, calling for help. Many perhaps are victims of their own youthful folly, or of their prolonged resistance to God's grace, or of sheer neglect of parental warnings, or of stubborn opposition to God's commands and the sane and saintly advice of zealous pastors of souls. Others again are lying by the wayside only partly through their own fault. They are blinded by inherited prejudice, or morally weakened by a bad upbringing, or have been victims of men's callous corrupting influence. Whatever the cause, it is the effect — the spiritually wounded lying helpless by life's roadside — which is calling on our charity.

The true Christian will find the time and the means to bring succor to those wounded souls. The oil of charity first, the word of comfort coming from a brother; the wine of advice and encouragement will follow; and later he will take the injured brother to Christ's innkeeper who will do the rest.

What a wonderful world this would be if only there were more good Samaritans traveling our way; if only there were more true followers of Christ who had their neighbor's spiritual and temporal well-being at heart.

Such good Samaritans are, alas, few and far between, but from today their ranks will be increased by one more — I will become, and remain, a good Samaritan.

Christian Humility

If charity or true brotherly love is the chief fruit of the Christian tree, one of the deepest and most essential roots of that tree is humility. Without that root the tree will wither and die. Without humility no Christian can claim to be following Christ. He came on earth — an act of humiliation so sublime that it staggers our imagination — in order to redeem us from the fatal effects of our first parents' proud disobedience. We had wandered far from God and Christ came to lead us back to our Father's home on the lowly path of humility. "Learn of me," He said, "because I am meek, and humble of heart" (Mt 11:29).

Our loving Savior taught us to be humble by word and example. His incarnation was an act of humility that can never be paralleled; His sojourn on earth was one continuous exercise of humiliation. "[He] emptied himself [of His divine prerogatives]," says St. Paul, "taking the form of a servant, being made in the likeness of men, in habit found as a man. He humbled himself, becoming obedient unto death, even to death on a cross" (Phil 2:7-8). Frequently, too, in His preaching He exhorted His disciples and all who would come after Him to practice this fundamental and essential virtue. The following parables, brief though they be, are lessons which we can ignore only at our peril.

THE LAST PLACE AT A FEAST

"And he spoke a parable also to them that were invited, marking how they chose the first seats at the table saying to them: When thou art invited to a wedding, sit not down in the first place, lest perhaps one more honourable than thou be invited by him: and he that invited thee and him, come and say to thee: Give this man place: and then thou begin with shame to take the lowest place. But when thou art invited, go, sit down in the lowest place: that when he who invited thee, cometh, he may say to thee: Friend, go up higher. Then shalt thou have glory before them that sit at table with thee. Because every one that exalteth himself, shall be humbled; and he that humbleth himself, shall be exalted" (Lk 14:7–11).

EXPLANATION: The occasion on which our Lord spoke this parable was the following: He had been invited to a meal in the house of a Pharisee, where many other Pharisees had gathered. The purpose of the invitation was to try to trap Jesus into doing or saying something with which they could accuse Him. It was a Sabbath day, and they had arranged that a man suffering from dropsy should appear suddenly in the dining room. To their way of thinking, this situation would embarrass Jesus in one of three ways: if He healed the sick man, they could accuse Him of violating the Sabbath; if He refused to cure him, He could and would be accused of lacking human compassion; if He were unable to cure him, which they thought was most likely, for dropsy was looked on then as an incurable disease, then they could accuse Him of being an imposter. Their stratagem failed. Our Lord healed the sick man and showed them that He knew the evil designs they had in their hearts, thus giving a double proof of His divine power.

Pride was the predominant vice of the Pharisees. In fact, pride was the chief cause of their opposition to Jesus. Even at a simple festivity like the present dinner, it shows its ugly head: each one is striving to have the first place or seat of honor next to the host. It is then our Lord proposes this simple, homely parable to the assembled company.

When thou are invited to a wedding: To take the sting out of His lesson, as it were, He mentions a wedding feast, thus excluding any allusion to the present occasion.

Sit not down in the first place: Meals were eaten in a reclining position in those days. We would say today: "Do not sit in the first place unless you are the principal guest, and have been placed there by your host."

Lest perhaps one more honorable: If you have taken the first place and the guest for whom that place was intended arrives, then you will really be embarrassed, for the host will ask you to vacate the place you have wrongly taken, and as all the other places are occupied by now, you will have to take the lowest place of all.

But . . . go, sit down in the lowest place: If no place has been assigned to you, choose the lowest, and if you are worthy of a higher place, your host will see to it that you get it; and so you will be honored in the presence of all the other guests.

Because every one who exalteth himself: This is the conclusion, both of the parable and of the incident that preceded it. The proud will bring embarrassment on themselves both in this life and the next, but it is with the embarrassment in the next life that our Lord is chiefly concerned. The proud Pharisees had planned to confound and humiliate Jesus in the presence of the bystanders by bringing a sick man into His presence on the Sabbath. They were the ones who were humiliated, for they were shown up in their true colors as evil schemers. In the parable He shows them how their pride may embarrass them in the presence of the other invited guests. It is in the next life that this saying of our Lord on humility is always and unfailingly fulfilled. In this life the proud frequently manage to "get away with it," and the humble are often left in the lowest places, but temporal rewards or temporal punishments are of small importance when compared with eternal.

APPLICATION: Humility ought to be the easiest virtue for a true Christian to practice. We know of God's love for us and of the infinite beneficence and mercy with which He treats us. And what can we do for Him in return? What gift of body or soul do we possess which we can call our own? What are we tiny creatures in the sight of God?

Think of the sublime example of divine humility that has been given us. The Son of God, Creator and Lord of the universe, was born in a stable; reared in the obscure village of Nazareth; earned His meager meals as a country carpenter; died on a cross as a public malefactor with two thieves as companions, and was buried in a stranger's grave. Could He have done more to induce us to listen to His counsel when He said, "Learn of me, for I am humble of heart"?

And yet there are Christians who are proud. They set themselves up as critics of God's wisdom: "Why should God do this to me?" "Why should God let this happen?" "Why should I have to struggle along in poverty?" "Why should my neighbor have only the good things of this world?" These are the questionings of a proud soul. Such Christians raise themselves above their neighbors in their own minds; they choose the first places; and from their self-appointed heights they look down on their fellow guests at God's banquet. One who acts in this fashion is hardly following the humble Christ. One who sets himself up as a judge of God or of his neighbor has not that essential Christian virtue, humility.

Pride prevented the Pharisees from accepting Christ. Pride made them exclude themselves from the kingdom of God. They had many good qualities, and they did many good works. But all the good they did was as an empty shell; its spiritual value, its inner substance, was corroded and eaten away by the woodworm of pride. We too must beware of this woodworm, this secret weapon of our archenemy Satan. A thorough sifting of the motives which inspire me in the carrying out of my spiritual duties, a clear scrutiny of my judgments on my neighbor, an honest examination of how I accept my place in God's plan, these will show me whether I am a follower of the proud Pharisees or a humble servant of Christ.

THE PHARISEE AND THE PUBLICAN

"And to some who trusted in themselves as just, and despised others, he spoke also this parable: Two men went up into the temple to pray: the one a Pharisee and the other a publican. The Pharisee standing, prayed thus with himself: O God, I give thee thanks that I am not as the rest of men, extortioners, unjust, adulterers, as also is this publican. I fast twice a week: I give tithes of all that I possess. And the publican, standing afar off, would not so much as lift up his eyes towards heaven; but struck his breast, saying: O God, be merciful to me, a sinner:

I say to you, this man went down into his house justified rather than the other: because every one that exalteth himself, shall be humbled: and he that humbleth himself, shall be exalted" (Lk 18:9–14).

EXPLANATION: This story or parable was told by our Lord in order to drive home the lesson that humility is the only basis on which our dealings with God can be built. God is infinitely good and infinitely merciful, but He is also infinitely just. He has given to man all the gifts of body and soul that he possesses. If man forgets this and takes to himself the credit and the honor for any good deeds he may do, he is dishonest. Pride is dishonesty, then, and cannot be tolerated by the infinitely just God.

The two characters introduced in the parable by our Lord to illustrate His lesson could not be better chosen. The Pharisees were the "saints" of that time — according to themselves. They looked down on everybody else. They alone were the only faithful followers of the law; they alone had a sure place in God's kingdom; all others were sinners and despised by God. The publicans, on the other hand, were regarded by all as the champion sinners of that era. They were men who, for a guaranteed sum, leased the collection of taxes of a certain district from the Roman government. It was up to them to collect that sum, and whatever they collected over and above that amount was their own personal gain. This inevitably led to extortion and oppression. Many of these tax-collectors were Jews, and were thus doubly hated by the people, for, as well as being extortioners, they were also renegades to their faith and to their fatherland, because they cooperated with the pagan Roman oppressors.

Our Lord has a Pharisee and a publican praying in the temple at Jerusalem. He describes their prayer and tells us what God thinks of each.

The Pharisee standing, prayed thus: The prayer of the Pharisee is that of a proud man, who takes credit for his own external good deeds, and condemns those who are not like himself.

O God, I give thee thanks that I am not as the rest of men: Thanking God for being a good-living man would be an excellent prayer if it were sincere, but it is evident here that this Pharisee is not sincere, for he takes the credit to himself and rashly judges all others. What his words really mean is: "O God, You should be thankful that You have a saint like me around. I deserve great credit, whereas these others are a blot on the face of the earth. Why do You tolerate them?"

Extortioners . . . adulterers: Injustice and impurity are sins against God's law, and there were many guilty of such sins then as now; but there was and there is a greater sin — the sin of pride, the sin committed by Satan in heaven, and by Adam, at the instigation of Satan, in Eden. The robber and the adulterer can admit their faults, and can ask their pardon and will receive it — the good thief and Mary Magdalen are proofs of this — but the truly proud cannot easily humble himself. God has pardon for all sins, but not all sinners will ask Him for pardon.

As also is this publican: In the mind of the Pharisee, the publican was a robber and an adulterer, but he was even worse, he was a heretic, for he associated with, and worked for, the pagan Romans. How rash was the Pharisee's judgment the sequel shows.

I fast twice a week: Having proudly disclaimed any taint of the human weaknesses that afflict other men, he goes on now to tell of the positive good works he does, for which God ought to be grateful. The law of Moses commanded fasting on one day of the year only — the Day of Atonement — but the Pharisees, on their own authority, introduced many other such days. However the observance was not obligatory, nor was it meritorious for those who boasted of having kept it. This habit of boasting of their so-called virtues, on the part of the

Pharisees, is condemned by our Lord in strong words, in Chapter 23 of St. Matthew's Gospel; and in Chapter 6 He tells His disciples: "And when you fast, be not as the hypocrites, sad. For they disfigure their faces, that they may appear unto men to fast. Amen I say to you, they have received their reward. But thou, when thou fastest anoint thy head, and wash thy face; that thou appear not to men to fast, but to thy Father who is in secret: and thy Father who seeth in secret, will repay thee" (16–18).

I give tithes: The Jews were bound to pay tithes, i.e., the tenth part of some of the annual produce of their land, their herds, and their flocks for the upkeep of the temple and the divine service. But the Pharisees tried to extend this tax to all possessions, and boasted of doing so themselves.

And the publican: What a contrast! The publican admits his guilt, he finds he has nothing to be proud of, but much to be ashamed of, and ashamed he is. "[He] would not so much as lift up his eyes towards heaven."

But struck his breast: An outward sign of his interior repentance and regret for his sins. This gesture was evidently fairly common among the Jews of that time. St. Luke tells us that the crowd that had witnessed the crucifixion of Jesus with its accompanying strange happenings, returned to the city from Calvary "beating their breasts." They felt a great crime had been committed by their leaders and themselves.

O God, be merciful to me, a sinner: A true and a sincere prayer. He admits he has sinned; he takes all the blame for his sins; he does not mention any good deeds done: his only hope of forgiveness is the infinite mercy of God. For this he humbly asks.

I say to you . . . went down into his house justified: Our Lord now tells us the answer to the prayers of the two men. The publican received mercy from God; his sincere confession and his true sorrow for his sins won for him a pardon from God.

Rather than the other: The other, the Pharisee, went back to his home burdened with the same serious sin of pride, and instead of obtaining pardon, his prayer had added sins of rash judgment and uncharitableness.

Everyone that exalteth himself: Our Lord gives the reason for the failure of the Pharisee's prayer, and for every other prayer made in like manner. The reason was pride. The Pharisee had set himself up as one whom God should appreciate; whereas anything good he had done should have been attributed to God, who gave him the power and the will to think and to do. He was humbled therefore; that is, he was cast down from his exalted pedestal and left with his sins. If this humbling would give him the virtue of true humility, all would eventually be well, but there is no indication that it did, nor is it likely when one is inflamed with a spiritual pride of this nature. On the other end of the scale we have the true humility of a real penitent. This humility enabled the publican to admit the depths of his own unworthiness in God's sight; it encouraged him to plead for mercy to the Father of mercy, and merited divine pardon. "This man went down into his house justified."

APPLICATION: The hypocrisy of the Pharisees, who put on a veneer of sanctity to cover up a heart corrupted by pride, caused the name "Pharisee" to become synonymous with hypocrite in all languages for all time. If anybody but the Son of God Himself painted the above picture of the Pharisee at prayer in God's house, we might be excused if we thought the picture overdrawn. But it comes from Him who is Truth Itself.

In uttering His "woes" against the Pharisees, and in telling the above story about one of them, our Lord's purpose was to warn all of us against this most ruinous of vices — pride. Pride was the first sin ever committed; pride is still Satan's secret weapon in his continual war against God's kingdom. It is a secret weapon because it can be so successfully camouflaged under the cloak of piety. That Pharisee did a lot of works which were good in themselves, and avoided a lot of sins, but pride gave him a wrong motive — the motive of self-glory — and so these works gave no honor or glory to God. Rather, they offended God.

I must be ever on my guard, then, lest this demon of pride should get into my soul and wreck all my spiritual efforts. A frequent check on my motives will keep me on the straight and narrow path of humility. Do I make a parade of my good deeds, or do I prefer to do them in secret? Do I like my neighbors to know that I do some extra penances, and do I look down my nose at those who do nothing out of the ordinary? Do I give as generously to charitable causes when no list of benefactors is published, or do I seek to head the published list? Do I willingly take part among the rank and file in parish activities, or do I always want to be the leader in such activities?

When I hear of others falling by the way, do I despise and condemn them offhand, or do I pray for their conversion, and thank God sincerely for having preserved me from such temptations? Do I always try to find an excuse or an extenuation of the faults of others, or have I excuses for my own faults only? Do I feel angry when I do not get sufficient recognition for my public works of charity, and feel hurt when others make the headlines? A straight answer to these questions will help me to discover whether my motive in all my religious activity is the honor and glory of God or my own glorification. In all my good works in the future, I will strive to keep self in the background, and bring God more and more into the picture. For He has told me: "He who humbles himself shall be exalted."

SECTION NINE

The Qualities of True Prayer

Our divine Lord prayed frequently. As God, He had no need to pray; He had all things in His power; but as man He needed to pray for us. He took our human nature in order to buy us back from the slavery of Satan and restore us to God, and He used that human nature, from the moment of His conception until the moment when He finally sacrificed it on the cross, for our salvation. Prayer was one of the ways in which He used His human faculties to placate the heavenly Father for the sins of man, and to obtain God's favors for fallen humanity. A secondary motive in His acts of praying was to set us an example that we too should pray to God, thereby adoring Him, thanking Him, begging Him for pardon and for the graces we need. This example was not given in vain; very soon His disciples noticed how devoutly, how recollectedly, how sincerely He prayed, and they were quickly filled with a desire to imitate Him. They therefore asked Him to teach them how to pray, a request He gladly granted when He taught them the Lord's Prayer.

And not only did He set them and us an example and compose a special formula of prayer that we could use, but He added many instructions on the essence and the qualities of true prayer. We have some of these instructions in the four parables that follow, namely, on the necessity of filial trust in God when praying, and of perseverance in our requests even when God seems indifferent not only to our temporal but even to our spiritual needs, and finally He shows us that no one, not even an enemy, should be excluded from our prayers.

FATHER AND SON

"And which of you, if he ask his father bread, will he give him a stone? or a fish, will he for a fish give him a serpent? Or if he shall ask an egg, will he reach him a scorpion? If you then, being evil, know how to give good gifts to your children, how much more will your Father from heaven give the good Spirit to them that ask him" (Lk 11:11-13).

EXPLANATION: This short parable occurs in St. Matthew's Gospel in the Sermon on the Mount. St. Luke places it immediately after the parable of the midnight petitioner, but its only connection with that parable is that both deal with prayer. In both Matthew and Luke it is preceded by the exhortation: "Ask, and it shall be given you: seek, and you shall find: knock, and it shall be opened to you. For every one that asketh, receiveth; and he that seeketh, findeth; and to him that knocketh, it shall be opened (Mt 7:7; Lk 11:9-10). In these words Christ gives a clear and definite guarantee that every sincere prayer will receive a sincere answer. The three words ask, seek, and knock are just three metaphors for the one single idea: make your petitions known to God. Our Lord tells His followers they must have absolute confidence in God when they pray, and the parable shows the reason for this confidence.

If he ask his father bread, will he give him a stone? No human father, unless he has completely lost all natural feelings, would hand a stone to his hungry child who was crying for bread. That would be hardhearted cruelty.

Or a fish, will he for a fish give him a serpent? The eel and the serpent may look somewhat alike, but the eel is edi-ble, the serpent is not. Deception is added to cruelty.

Or if he shall ask an egg, will he reach him a scorpion? There are white scorpions in Palestine, but otherwise there is no similarity between a scorpion and an egg. But a child could be deceived and take the poisonous scorpion in its hand. This act of a father would not only be cruel and deceptive, but would show murderous intent.

If you then, being evil: If finite human nature, even in its fallen sinful state, is such that one cannot even imagine a father treating his child in this manner . . .

How much more will your Father from heaven: How infinitely more impossible is it that the heavenly Father, who is infinitely perfect, infinitely good, and infinitely powerful, could answer his children's requests with cruel, deceptive, injurious gifts? Instead, he will:

Give the good Spirit to them that ask him: The Holy Spirit is the Source of all blessed gifts, temporal and spiritual. Our kind Father, who loves us with a love immeasurably greater than the love of all earthly fathers put together, will send down from heaven to those who ask Him not only all the blessings, temporal and spiritual, that they need, but the very Source and Fountain of these blessings, the Holy Spirit Himself.

APPLICATION: A true, childlike confidence in God is the first requisite for all successful prayer of petition. This is what our divine Lord teaches us in this parable; this is what He meant when He placed in the forefront of the prayer He Himself gave us, the phrase "Our Father, who art in heaven." God, the Lord of heaven and earth, is our Father, a Father who has a particular and personal interest in each one of us, an interest which went to such an extreme of love that He sent His only-begotten, divine Son on earth to redeem us — to buy us back — by His sufferings and death, after we had left Him through Adam's sin. Such is God in relation to us. He is not just a supreme, omnipotent Being who resides in inaccessible glory, far removed from transient, finite, frail mankind. He is not merely the omniscient, all-wise Creator who set the world in motion and guides it with the unerring, ironclad laws of immutable justice. Nor is He merely the all-perfect, remote Ruler who exacts unconditional obedience from servile subjects; but He is, instead, a FATHER who loves each one of us, and wants to share with us His patrimony of eternal and infinite happiness. God is our Father! God is my Father! What a staggering thought, when I think of what I am, but what a consoling and strengthening thought when I realize what it can mean to me.

When I come to God to place my requests before Him, I come not as a servant to his master, not as a subject to his king, not as a friend seeking a favor from a fellow man, but as a son to his father — a Father who is not only capable of granting all my requests, but infinitely willing to do so, provided they are for my ultimate benefit. The human father described in the parable would cease to be a human and a father if he refused to give to his son the necessities of life he asked for; the divine Father cannot cease to be divine, or a Father, once He has adopted us as His sons, and therefore will never refuse our lawful requests. The human father's will to help his son is limited by the finite means at his disposal; the divine Father's power is infinite, and His will to help unlimited. Therefore — and this is the lesson of Christ's parable — we, His adopted sons, should approach God our Father with absolute trust, placing our needs before Him, supremely confident that He can and will grant our requests.

But it will be objected, if absolute filial confidence and trust is all that is needed on our part in order to get our lawful requests from God, how do so many fervent prayers go unanswered? Leaving aside for a moment the question of perseverance in prayer, which will be dealt with in the next parable, let us examine the two suppositions underlying this objection, namely, that there is absolute filial trust on the part of the petitioners, and that their requests are "lawful," that is, for and not against the ultimate good of those making the requests of God. To approach God with a true filial trust and confidence presupposes a firm conviction that we are God's children, and that our one and only real purpose in life is to serve Him on earth in order to share infinite happiness with Him in heaven. The proof of this firm conviction will be our daily mode of living, our outlook on life, for such a conviction will influence all our actions. Can the worldly-minded man or woman whose thoughts and aims are earth-bounded, and who thinks of God only when in some serious need of a temporal favor — can such a petitioner suddenly become a true, loving child of God, deserving of all the paternal solicitude of the eternal Father? If the prodigal son had written to his father for a further donation in order to continue living wantonly away from home in open defiance of his father's will, would anyone really be surprised if the good father had not sent the money by return mail? The prayers of sinners, it is true, have been answered again and again, but only when they turned from their sin and became repentant but true children of God. The prodigal got a royal welcome when, and because, he came home. True filial trust in the fatherhood of God is not something that can be put on and off like a change of clothing. It is part of a man's life; it affects his whole outlook and manner of living. No amount of fervor and earnestness on our part when entreating our heavenly Father for some sorely needed help will make us dutiful, trusting children unless we already are such or here and now definitely break with our past and sincerely resolve to be such from now on.

The absence of the second necessary condition of a worthy prayer, namely, the lawfulness of the request, may explain God's refusal in very many cases too. Many a loving, kind earthly father has granted the apparently reasonable request of his dutiful son, only to live to regret it all his life. Such a father's knowledge was limited; he could not foresee the future. The heavenly Father cannot and does not act in this manner. He loves His children; He knows what is for their ultimate good and what is not. Because He is a loving Father with a true interest in His child, He does not grant any favor that would be injurious to that child. We, His children, may feel grieved and even dissatisfied at times with His manner of treating us, but this is only because our limited human minds cannot see beyond our immediate surroundings. We see only the need of the moment. God has the overall plan of our lives before His eyes.

Let us face facts. With the exception of those devout generous souls who gladly and deliberately choose the road of sufferings and hardships, the vast majority of mankind, fervent, faithful Christians included, would like to get to heaven by the easiest and least exacting route. And so it happens that of every thousand prayers of petition addressed to God, nine hundred and ninety-nine are asking to have some cross removed; the solitary exception is that of the saint asking for a new cross. If you were in God's place and knew that the cross was the very means by which weak, mean human nature could be raised above itself and made worthy of the eternal happiness of heaven, would you or could you grant these requests?

Yet God does answer all sincere prayers. The very favor asked for is often granted when it is in conformity with God's all-wise plan, but where this is withheld a greater and a bigger gift is given in its stead. A glance at almost any page of the history of God's dealings with the human race will prove this. If the devout prayers of Jacob had been answered directly, his beloved son Joseph would not have been sold into slavery in Egypt by his wicked brothers. Yet the slavery of Joseph turned out to be the salvation of Jacob and those wicked brothers. If the pious youth Daniel had been spared the sufferings of his captivity in Babylon, what a spiritual loss not only the Chosen People and Christians would have suffered, but his very persecutors the Babylonians themselves. Surely the mothers of Bethlehem called on God to save their little innocents from the cruelty of Herod, and great indeed was their heartbreak when their prayers failed, as they thought, but today, looking down from the heaven which their martyred children earned for them, are they thankful to God He did not remove the cross? All of the twelve Apostles, except John, were struck down more or less in the prime of life by cruel persecutors. What millions of fervent prayers went up to God from the faithful converts asking Him to spare the Apostles to carry on their great work for souls, yet their very martyrdom proved more effective for spreading the faith than another sixty years of their inspired preaching would have been.

"Ask, and it shall be given to you," our Lord tells us, not "you may be given." He tells us to ask, and He guarantees an answer, an answer in many cases far more useful than the particular favor we sought. Let us approach God, then, as dutiful children, coming to a benevolent Father in all our needs, temporal and spiritual. We know He is able and is willing to help us on our journey through life. Remember, he will never give us a stone if bread is what we need, but we, in our ignorance, may be asking for a stone. A loving Father will put it beyond our reach, and will give us the bread we did not ask for.

PERSEVERANCE IN PRAYER

We saw in the preceding parable that God always answers the sincere prayers of His faithful children, and the clear unequivocal statement of Christ: "Ask, and it shall be given to you" is proof of this. The answer, however, is not always the one requested, and hence it is not always recognized as an answer. The mothers of Bethlehem surely must have thought that God had turned a deaf ear to their heartrending cries, although he was giving them an infinitely greater gift than that asked for — unending happiness and eternal life, when they had asked for a few years of doubtful earthly happiness for their loved ones. Furthermore, the direct answer, though frequently given, is often delayed for God's all-wise reasons; the very delay is part of His plan. But unfortunately we cannot always see this, and consequently we are strongly tempted to suspect that God is indifferent to our prayers and not interested in our welfare.

Life on earth is, for the vast majority, one long continual struggle against overwhelming odds. Buffeted and bruised by the storms and tempests of life, an innocent helpless victim often of both the unruly processes of nature and the injustices of his fellow man, it is small wonder if the man of weak faith and of little knowledge of God should deny His existence. Yet the loving hand of God is as much present in the storm as in the calm. A mother loves her child as much when giving him unpleasant but necessary medicine as when giving him a spoon of honey. Does the child realize this? No, just because he is a child. We are children, and very small children, in relation to God, and therefore we are apt to misjudge His providence and to see harshness and neglect instead of solicitude.

That astounding act of love — the Incarnation — whereby the Son of God came down on earth to live a life of hardship and humiliation among us and die an excruciating and ignominious death on the cross, should be proof convincing to any open mind of God's infinite love for us.

The following two parables were spoken by our Lord with this very purpose in view, to stress namely the truth that God is supremely willing to help us in our needs, even on those occasions when to all external appearances He seems to be completely impervious to our entreaties. These two parables are an exposition of the introductory words of the second parable: "We ought always to pray, and not to faint" (Lk 18:1); that is, we must retain all our confidence in the loving goodness of our heavenly Father and continue to tell Him of our needs even and especially when He seems to be least attentive to our plea.

Although both parables treat of the same theme, there is a shade of difference: in the midnight petitioner, the neighbor has no obligation in justice to help his needy friend, but the judge of the second parable is in justice bound to hear the widow's plea. We shall apply the first parable to requests for temporal favors, the granting of which depends entirely on God's infinite generosity; the second shall be applied to spiritual favors, to which we, as adopted children of God, have a certain right, if not in strict justice, at least as a consequence of the first great grace of adoption given us by God.

THE MIDNIGHT PETITIONER

"And he said to them: Which of you shall have a friend, and shall go to him at midnight, and shall say to him: Friend, lend me three loaves. Because a friend of mine is come off his journey to me, and I have not what to set before him. And he from within should answer, and say: Trouble me not, the door is now shut, and my children are with me in bed; I cannot rise and give thee. Yet if he shall continue knocking, I say to you, although he will not rise and give him, because he is his friend; yet, because of his importunity, he will rise, and give him as many as he needeth" (Lk 11:5–8).

EXPLANATION: To our Lord's listeners, every detail of this story was familiar. The incident as narrated could have happened to any of them, and indeed it still happens today to the poor in most parts of the world. A friend or relative turns up at the very moment when some essential ingredient of a meal is missing. The solution to the problem is — especially if the stores are closed — go and borrow from a neighbor.

A friend . . . is come . . . to me: He was unexpected, but not unwelcome. He was tired and hungry after a long journey, and his host was anxious to be hospitable, but he found himself in an embarrassing situation. He had not the wherewithal to place a meal before his guest. He had no bread, the staple food then, as today, in Palestine. This was not necessarily a sign of his extreme poverty. Each village had its communal oven, and each housewife had her allotted time in which to use it. The housewives usually baked sufficient bread to last their families a few days or more. It just happened that this household had used up its supply when the visitor arrived; but they had a friend whose wife had baked a new batch of bread that day. To this friend the man goes, full of confidence that his problem will be quickly solved.

Friend, lend me three loaves: This mutual borrowing of urgent family needs was common practice, and were the hour more reasonable the request would probably have been granted immediately. But it was midnight, and the friend was any-thing but pleased at having his sleep disturbed.

Trouble me not, the door is now shut: The answer from within was not at all friendly. Being awakened from sleep at this hour was most annoying, and any feeling of friendship that had hitherto existed was now frozen cold.

My children are with me in bed: The normal home of the poor and middle-class people consisted of one room. The family slept on mats on the floor, huddled close together to keep warm. To reach the door, the father would have to step over his sleeping children in the dark. The probability that he would accidentally step on one of them, thus causing an outcry which would awaken the whole family, was something to be dreaded; hence this added excuse for his reluctance to help his friend.

I cannot rise and give thee: The matter should and would have ended there, if the friend outside were less determined.

If he shall continue knocking: But this friend continued to bang on the door. In the silence of the night, and to the taut nerves of the householder, this knocking sounds like a demolition squad wielding sledgehammers. Any moment the children would be awake, and the catastrophe he hoped to avoid by not rising would have happened anyway. So

Because of his importunity: He will arise and give the loaves to the neighbor, if not out of love and friendship, at least in order to avoid a greater evil — the awakening of the children.

APPLICATION: Our Lord wished to teach His disciples, and, through them, all of us, the necessity of persevering in prayer if we want to have our requests granted. As in all His parables the illustration He uses here is homely and effective. If a human friend who has a hundred excuses for turning a deaf ear to his petitioner is forced to grant a request because of the perseverance and importunity of that petitioner, how much more so will the one and only true friend of man be moved to answer the requests of those who persevere in asking?

If perseverance, then, can force a fellow man, whose friendship at the best of times is riddled with selfishness and many other human weaknesses, to grant our request, how much more effectively will that same perseverance work on the all-loving Father in heaven, who has no weakness and whose sole desire is to help us in our need? But here one may well ask: Why does God demand perseverance from us; why does He not grant immediately what we ask for; and for that matter, why does He not give what we need without our asking for it? The fact is, of course, that He does give us 99 per cent of our needs of soul and body without our asking for them. He gave us our existence, which means our immortal soul with its quasi-divine faculties of intellect and free will, and a body which will be immortal after the general resurrection. He gave us the infused virtues of faith, hope, and charity in baptism. He gave us His Church to help us on the road to the eternal happiness He has prepared for us. In fine, He gave us freely everything we are and can be. But because we have free will, which raises us above all other earthly creatures and makes us human beings, He must let us choose freely to follow the path to eternal happiness he has mapped out for us. As this path is supernatural, above our ordinary human powers, we need His supernatural help on every step of the road; this is the 1 per cent He tells us to ask for. This is the means He has devised in His infinite wisdom and love to enable us to "earn" heaven. Could any person of sound mind who has even an elementary grasp of God and self say that God is overexacting in asking this much of him?

Suppose for a moment you have to travel from New York to San Francisco. A friend gives you a gift of a brand-new automobile to take you there. Not only that, but he has mapped out the safest and the best route for you, and has arranged with service stations and restaurants along that route to supply you with gasoline and everything you need on the way. All you have to do is follow the route and call at the service stations. Would you consider the friend exacting because you had to follow the route he has chosen and stop at these stations to pick up the supplies he had prepared for you? This is exactly how God deals with us. He has given us freely all the essentials for our safe journey to heaven, He has laid down the route we should follow, He asks us to stop at the service stations He has indicated, to collect, by just asking for them, the daily needs our journey requires. This is what He taught us when He told us to say: "Give us this day our daily bread."

And our "daily bread" includes our temporal needs as well as our spiritual ones. We travel to heaven in and with our body; the needs of the body are an essential part of our equipment for the journey. It is therefore not only lawful for us to ask God for these needs, it is obligatory that we should do so. This is His own command, and the history of His dealings with man proves that such requests will not go unanswered. The very first miracle performed by Christ was worked in Cana to relieve a temporal need. We must pray then for our material or bodily needs, and the lesson our Lord teaches us in this parable is that we must persevere in our prayers even when the odds seem to be stacked against us. Through such perseverance we prove our filial trust in our heavenly Father, and our true loyalty to our divine King. We all know from experience how easy it is to forget God and our eternal destiny when all is going well, but our loving Father has His corrective for that human weakness. He sends His periodic reminders in the form of bodily ailments, financial and other needs in order to recall His children's minds to the true realities of life. Temporal crosses are God's way of keeping us close to Him. Life on earth is not our end in itself, but it leads to our real end; it is a journey to our final goal. Like all journeys, it is hard and difficult, but these drawbacks are the very means we must use to ensure safe arrival at our destination.

It is God's will, then, that we should pray to Him in all our temporal needs, and that we should persevere in our prayer. An answer He always gives. When He delays the granting of the bread, for example, it is because the acts of religion elicited in our perseverance in prayer are more essential to us than the material favor we are seeking here and now. When He seems to refuse to open the door of his mercy to us, it is because our continued knocking will be of greater help to us in our journey to heaven than the three loaves we came to seek. The loaves, too, we shall get eventually, but in the meantime, if we persevere in prayer, we shall receive greater favors for which we had not asked, and which perhaps we did not even know we needed.

THE UNJUST JUDGE

"And he spoke also a parable to them, that we ought always to pray, and not to faint. Saying: There was a judge in a certain city, who feared not God, nor regarded man. And there was a certain widow in the city, and she came to him, saying: Avenge me of my adversary. And he would not for a long time. But afterwards he said within himself: Although I fear not God, nor regard man, yet because this widow is troublesome to me, I will avenge her lest continually coming she weary me. And the Lord said: Hear what the unjust judge saith. And will not God revenge his elect who cry to him day and night: and will he have patience in their regard? I say to you, that he will quickly revenge them. But yet the Son of man when he cometh, shall he find, think you, faith on earth?" (Lk 18:1–8).

EXPLANATION: To show the necessity and effectiveness of perseverance in prayer, our Lord chose this second parable or illustration, in which perseverance produces results in the most unlikely circumstances.

There was a judge: Every town and larger village of Palestine had a magistrate or official appointed by the central authority, whose duty it was to decide all local quarrels and solve questions of disputed rights after hearing both sides.

Who feared not God, nor regarded man: A more unsuitable man for this responsible position could not be found. He "feared not God"; that is, he ignored God and His law; he was a nonpracticing Jew (a pagan would not be accused of not fearing God, for he was ignorant of the true God) to whom the ten commandments meant nothing; neither did human respect bother him, for he ignored and despised the opinions of his fellow men and went his own sweet way, a law unto himself. That such a description is not the mere literary invention of our Lord we know from the Talmud, which gives many examples of the glaring injustices committed by venal and corrupt magistrates, especially in the smaller towns and villages of the period. Nor was this a result of the Roman occupation, for we find the prophet Isaias, centuries previously, denouncing the unjust judges "That justify the wicked for gifts, and take away the justice of the just from him" (Is 5:23), and to Israel he said: "Thy princes are faithless, companions of thieves, they all love bribes, they run after rewards. They judge not for the fatherless: and the widow's cause cometh not in to them" (Is 1:23). So the judge in this parable was not exactly a stranger to our Lord's listeners.

There was a certain widow in the city: The very name "widow" conjures up a vision of one weak and helpless. She was a woman who had lost her protector and her breadwinner, and had now to take the place of father and mother in bringing up the family. She of all people needed charity, kindness, and justice. God frequently reminded His Chosen People in the Old Testament of the obligation toward widows and orphans (cf. Ex 22:22; Dt 14:29; 16:11, 14; 24:17; Is 1:23; Jb 22:9; etc.), and this exhortation was very necessary, for then as now there were those who were unscrupulous enough to rob the weak. This particular widow was one such; she had been robbed of a right by some neighbor or relative. Very probably some property willed to her by her late husband had been taken from her by one of his relatives, an act as inhuman as it was unjust.

She came to him: Her appeals to the justice and humanity of her despoiler were in vain, so she had recourse to the town magistrate whose duty it was to see that justice was done.

Avenge me of my adversary: The original Greek for "avenge" has two meanings: to "obtain justice" and to "punish the evildoer." That the poor widow's interest was to obtain justice, to get back her property or right, rather than the punishment of her opponent, can hardly be questioned. A just judge would see to the punishment of the guilty also, but her purpose in appealing to the magistrate was to recover what was hers in justice.

And he would not for a long time: This unscrupulous man refused again and again to listen to the widow's case; but she was evidently not going to admit defeat, for "she kept coming to him," as the Greek text has it. Against this unjust and unworthy magistrate, the only resource she had left was stubborn perseverance. And this she used effectively.

Afterwards he said within himself: The widow's perseverance gradually ("afterwards" = after a while) wore him down, and he had to admit that he was beaten.

Although I fear not God, nor regard man: He admits to himself that even though he despises God and man, yet he cannot continue to despise this woman, and must give judgment in her favor, not out of a sense of duty, but

Lest continually coming she weary me: Her continued perseverance was more than he could bear, and the longer it went on the more it affected him. The Greek word for "weary" is much stronger in its literal sense; it means "to give one a black eye," "to beat one black and blue." But it is just the type of exaggeration one would expect a character such as this magistrate to use. It is highly improbable that he expected or feared physical violence from a poor helpless widow, but her continual knocking on his door was to his selfish mind as unbearable and injurious as a physical beating.

I will avenge her: Forced by the utter determination of the defenseless widow, the unjust judge heard her case and gave legal sanction to her just claim.

And the Lord said: Hear what the unjust judge saith: Our Lord Himself applies the parable. If a man as wicked as the judge described above is moved by the persistent request of a helpless widow to listen to her plea, how much more certain is it that God, who is not only all-just, but all-kind and all-merciful as well, will listen to those who appeal to Him if they prove by their perseverance that their approach to Him is filial and sincere?

Will not God revenge his elect. . . ? "Elect" is another name for the followers of Christ, also frequently called "the saints" by St. Paul (cf. Rom 1:7; 12:13; etc.), that is, the chosen people of the

New Testament. The term "saints" does not mean that they already possess all virtues in an heroic degree, but that God has given them the call to election and sanctity — they are on the road to heaven; but they must "with fear and trembling work out [their] salvation" (Phil 2:12). This very verse proves this, for God's elect are in need of His assistance, and our Lord promises that God will avenge them; that is, He will hear their cry for help and will give the decision in their favor against the adversary who is trying to despoil them of their claim to heaven. As in the case of the widow, who was not asking the judge to punish her adversary, but rather to give back to her the property taken unjustly from her, so also with the elect it is not a case of God punishing their enemy, but rather of preventing him from impeding them on their road to heaven.

Who cry to him day and night: But the necessary condition for God's intervention on their behalf is their constant perseverance in prayer.

Will he have patience in their regard?: Will He delay unduly the aid they are seeking; will He tolerate for too long the actions of the adversary, as the unjust judge was disposed to do? It may and does often seem so to His elect, but that is because man's ideas of delay and immediacy are not those of God.

I say to you, that he will quickly revenge them: Christ answers the question He put above. God will quickly avenge them. But how does this quick response fit in with the perseverance, the protracted "day and night" prayer demanded by the parable? Again it is a question of our idea of immediacy and God's idea. If God did our will, all our temptations and trials would end as soon as they begin. We would all run to heaven, we think, if all obstacles were removed from our path; but God knows better and acts accordingly. The lordly oak does not grow in a balmy southern climate; the victorious soldier is not the product of a luxurious drawing room; so too, the storms and battles of life are necessary to form the elect of God, the saints of heaven. The very delay is part of God's answer to prayer; the perseverance He demands is a necessary constituent of our spiritual formation. His answer is "quick" because it comes at the right moment.

Son of man when he cometh: Many authors doubt if this phrase is to be connected with the preceding parable, but this is perhaps because they understand the coming of the Son of man as referring to the second coming at the end of the world. "The Son of man when he cometh" can refer also to any special intervention of Christ (as the distributer of God's mercy) in human affairs. Here it can mean "when at the appointed time God will answer the prayer of the oppressed."

Shall he find, think you, faith on earth? How many will have continued trusting in Him, how many will have persevered in their prayer? This is put in the form of a question by our Lord to His audience. It is not casting a doubt on the number that will persevere, but is rather a deduction which the audience should draw from the parable; that is, all should persevere even if their case seems hopeless. All those who truly believe that God is their kind Father should answer: "We will persevere, for we know He will intervene in His own good time."

APPLICATION: There are many good, devout people who are willing enough to admit that God is all-wise and all-kind to us even when He refuses our requests for temporal favors, but who are ready to question His wisdom and His kindness when He seems to ignore our appeals for spiritual favors essential for our journey toward salvation. Why, they ask, should souls dedicated to God's exclusive service by the vows of religion be still subject to the assaults of the world, the flesh, and the devil, or why should their efforts for their own and others' salvation be crippled by doubts and scruples when God could so easily grant them relief from such fettering handicaps by speedily answering their piteous pleas? Or why should whole nations of God's elect be crushed beneath the tyrannous heels of Satan's human agents, notwithstanding the fervent prayers for help sent up daily to God by the faithful of the world on their behalf? Or again, why should the self-sacrificing endeavors of generous missionaries be thwarted or in many cases reduced to naught by evil men when a speedy answer to the prayers of these missionaries and their benefactors, for the spread of God's kingdom, could so easily remove the obstacles that block their way?

These and a hundred other similar questions come to our minds because our limited intellects can see but one small section of the immense tapestry which God is weaving for the human race. We want immediate results in our own tiny corner of that tapestry, while the all-knowing God is occupied with the whole picture. We are anxious to see and to reap an abundant harvest from what we have sown, while God's plan for us is that we should only sow, or perhaps only prepare the ground for sowing, and leave the reaping to others. What to us finite creatures appear as huge obstacles are but helpful stepping-stones to the infinite God; what we may consider wasted endeavor and defeat is in God's plan the deep and solid foundation of a great triumph.

It is for this very reason, namely, that our finite intellect cannot see the lofty mountains because of the little foothills that surround us, that our Lord stressed so much our need of patience and perseverance. We must continue "to do what in us lies," even when to all external appearances God does not seem to be doing His part. If we did but realize it, God is never closer to us than when we feel He has abandoned us. The spiritual and temporal trials of life are God's loving way of forming us into worthy citizens of heaven. If we accept these trials and continue to trust in the kindness and love of our heavenly Father, we shall one day come to realize that the fervent prayers we poured out for the removal of our crosses were answered in a way infinitely more beneficial to us than we ever dreamed of, just because God loves us.

The unjust judge eventually granted the widow's request because of her perseverance. The all-just and all-loving God is answering our prayer every step of the way, not always by removing the obstacles which threaten to impede our progress, but rather by giving us the strength to utilize these very obstacles to raise us up to the eternal victory for which He has destined us.

THE BARREN FIG TREE

"He spoke also this parable: A certain man had a fig tree planted in his vineyard, and he came seeking fruit on it, and found none. And he said to the dresser of the vineyard: Behold, for these three years I come seeking fruit on this fig tree and I find none. Cut it down therefore: why encumbereth it the ground? But he answering, said to him: Lord, let it alone this year also, until I dig about it, and dung it. And if happily it bear fruit: but if not, then after that thou shalt cut it down" (Lk 13:6–9).

EXPLANATION: In the preceding discourse (12:23–30) our Lord had warned the Pharisees that the fact that they were children of Abraham and members of the Chosen People — a fact of which they continually boasted — was far from being a guarantee that the kingdom of heaven was theirs. Their father and founder, Abraham, had been chosen by God to found a nation which would keep the knowledge of the true God alive in a world of pagans until such time as He would send the Redeemer promised to Adam after the fall. This Redeemer, called by the prophets "the Messias," that is, the anointed King, Priest, and

Prophet of God, would come from this chosen nation. To preserve the knowledge of the true God and to prepare for the coming of the Messias was the sole reason of their election as the Chosen People, but while they boasted of this privilege they had gradually come to forget and ignore the obligations this privilege laid on them. These leaders of the Jewish nation, the Pharisees, refused to accept Christ when He came, because He did not fulfill their ideas of what He should be. They wanted a political leader who would miraculously crush all their enemies, publicans, sinners, and pagans, and set up a temporal kingdom of power, wealth, and worldly glory for them. Instead, Christ preached a spiritual kingdom which was open to all who repented, pagans and sinners, and promised His followers earthly trials and tribulations rather than worldly wealth and glory. Again and again Christ reminded them of their wrong, worldly outlook, and sought to recall their minds to the things of God, the kingdom of heaven, which He had come on earth to found in their midst. This parable is one such reminder.

A certain man had a fig tree planted in his vineyard: The fig tree and the vines were the most commonly cultivated and most productive fruit trees in Palestine. The fig trees were planted in the vineyard, and as well as producing their own valuable fruit served as supports for the vine branches. Like the vines, they required annual pruning and care.

He came seeking fruit on it, and found none: The owner of the vineyard had done all that was expected of him for his tree, but in vain.

He said to the dresser of the vineyard: The dresser was the steward or manager who took charge of the vineyard and saw to its proper upkeep for the owner.

For these three years . . . I find none: The owner had already proved himself patient with this tree. A young tree which has reached the fruit-bearing age and fails two years in succession to fructify, or an old one which has ceased for two years to bear fruit, is usually cut down; this tree had already been given an extra chance, but it had failed a third time; therefore

Why encumbereth it the ground?: It had proved itself unworthy of further consideration, and must give place to a tree which would fulfill its purpose in life, namely, to produce fruit.

Lord, let it alone this year also: The steward of the vineyard interceded for this tree, asking for one year more of grace.

Until I dig about it, and dung it: He would give it very special care this year, in the hope that

Happily it bear fruit: Perhaps it would react to the special treatment and save itself from destruction.

If not, then . . . thou shalt cut it down: If it failed to avail itself of this last chance, then the master's will must be carried out.

APPLICATION: This parable was spoken, in the first instance, to the Pharisees and for the Pharisees, and they could hardly fail to see its implication. The Chosen People, Israel, was often described in the Old Testament under the image of God's vineyard (cf. Is 5:1–17), in which were His fig trees and vines. God in His mercy had spared them many a time when they merited extermination, but they continued to abuse His mercy and failed to produce the fruits of sincere repentance expected of them. John the Baptist had already warned them to stop boasting of Abraham, and to do works of penance. Using the same image as this parable, he said: "The axe is laid to the root of the trees. Every tree therefore that bringeth not forth good fruit, shall be cut down and cast into the fire" (Lk 3:9). But they did not heed John, and went on their sinful way abusing the extraordinary toleration which God's mercy had shown them. Christ now reminds them, in this parable, that their continued infidelity and their spiritual barrenness had already exhausted God's patience; but He Himself, the steward of the divine vineyard, had pleaded for them and had obtained one last opportunity of bringing forth "fruits worthy of penance"; one further year of reprieve has been granted the barren fig tree of Israel. Did they avail themselves of this last act of divine mercy? The parable does not answer this question because the issue was still undecided when our Lord spoke this parable; the decision was up to the Pharisees. Christ had done His part; would they do theirs? History has given the answer: many Pharisees did turn to Christ after His resurrection, but as a body they continued to oppose Him. Thus, they became like Cain, "a fugitive and a vagabond . . . upon the earth" (Gn 4:12).

There are precious lessons in this parable for all of us. For the obstinate sinner there is the dire warning that even though God's mercy is infinite the life of the sinner on earth is far from infinite and his time for repentance therefore limited. If he foolishly perseveres in his resistance to God's offers of pardon he will find himself cut off from that mercy by death; like Dives, he will realize his folly when it is too late. But of this the sinner may be assured, before that point is reached God's messengers of mercy will give him numerous warnings. No man has ever, and no man ever will lose his eternal happiness through invincible ignorance. He loses it through deliberately ignoring God's calls to repentance. These calls take many shapes and forms; they come at the most likely and unlikely times and places; woe to the sinner who continues to ignore these offers of divine mercy! Like the tree in the parable I may be on my last chance at this very moment. My sins may already have earned for me that I be cut off from God's elect, my span of life may be near its end, but the merciful Savior is offering me this last plank of salvation. I am free to accept or reject it; God cannot force my will. On my decision hangs an eternity.

Another important lesson which every true follower of Christ must learn from this parable is his obligation not only to forgive his enemies, but to pray to God that He too will forgive them. Our divine Lord, steward of God's vineyard, asked and obtained a further reprieve for the condemned fig tree — the Pharisees. These same Pharisees were his archenemies, determined to destroy Him and His kingdom, yet He pleaded with His heavenly Father to give them one more chance. In His divine knowledge He foresaw that their stubborn pride and prejudice would lead them on to the terrible crime of Calvary, with all the torments and tortures it entailed for Him. Yet in spite of all this, His chief concern was that they should escape the just punishment of their crimes. This is the headline He wishes His followers to copy.

But how difficult it is to copy this headline we all know from experience. And how few there are who really imitate our Lord in this is only too evident from the divisions and the dissensions that exist between neighbors and nations today. Fraternal charity has not only grown cold, for too many it has ceased to exist. The law of talion, "an eye for an eye and a tooth for a tooth," has returned among us to oust the command of brotherly love. The utopia dreamed up by vain materialistic philosophers, a brave new world in which all men are equal and supreme legislators of their own fate, has produced its natural fruit, the law of the jungle, man eats man. In a society where God is ignored and insulted there can be no true brotherhood of man. To forgive one's enemy and to ask God's pardon for that enemy's sinful deed is not the act of a mere human, it is the act of one raised above his earthly nature by the grace of God and by a supernatural belief in an eternal destiny for the human race. Every true Christian has this supernatural belief, and the grace of God is there for the asking.

Why is it, then, that so many Christians fail not only to pray for their enemies, but even refuse to forgive them, and will not rest until they have avenged the injury done them? Christianity for many, alas, is but a name and not a way of life. A theoretical abstract acceptance of the truths of the faith is not enough to make one a Christian. Christianity is a practical way of life, something in which one "lives, moves, and has one's being." Thus, the realization which the true Christian has of his own frailty, his own meanness, his own selfishness in the sight of God, gives him a deep understanding of the faults of his fellow man and a readiness to forgive. His deep appreciation of God's kindness and mercy as experienced by himself makes him of necessity kind and merciful to his neighbor.

We must then strive to be merciful as our heavenly Father is merciful. This requires a supernatural effort which comes only from a daily living of the Christian life, a constant realization of our heavenly destiny. Our home is heaven, we are on our way there; our neighbors on earth are all God's children and our brothers, and they too are on their way to heaven. We can and must help them. We are all weak and will fail and injure ourselves many times on our journey; we all need the divine Physician. His readiness to help will depend on our generosity in helping others: "In what measure you shall mete, it shall be measured to you" (Mk 4:24). God will reward all acts of fraternal charity, but He will especially reward the generous souls who, forgetful of self, promptly come to the aid of their fellow man who has injured them. This is true love of God and neighbor. This is how our Lord reacted to the evil-minded Pharisees. This is one of the lessons we must try to learn from this parable.

Heaven, the Generous Gift of God

Christ our Redeemer not only reopened heaven to us by His death on the cross, but He generously gave us all the means necessary for getting there. He has marked out the route we ought to follow, and He has provided the necessary supplies for the trip. He has given us His official representatives to lead, instruct, and encourage us on our journey. The part we have to play in getting to heaven is merely that we make use of the gifts of nature and of grace He has given us. These factors may impose some restrictions on selfish human nature, but what sane man would risk reaching a destination such as heaven because of such relatively trivial restrictions? And yet, unfortunately, some people will forfeit their eternal happiness for a few short years of personal pride, profit, or pleasure on this earth. The very talents God gave them to acquire true happiness in heaven, they squander in their search on earth for a happiness which does not exist. This is the teaching of the following parables, in which the folly of such failures, as well as the littleness of the efforts demanded of those who succeed in comparison with the reward, is clearly set forth.

THE POUNDS

"As they were hearing these things, he added and spoke a parable, because he was nigh to Jerusalem, and because they thought that the kingdom of God should immediately be manifested. He said therefore: A certain nobleman went into a far country, to receive for himself a kingdom, and to return. And calling his ten servants, he gave them ten pounds, and said to them: Trade till I come. But his citizens hated him: and they sent an embassage after him, saying: We will not have this man to reign over us. And it came to pass, that he returned, having received the kingdom: and he commanded his servants to be called, to whom he had given the money, that he might know how much every man had gained by trading. And the first came, saying: Lord, thy pound hath gained ten pounds. And he said to him: Well done, thou good servant, because thou hast been faithful in a little, thou shalt have power over ten cities. And the second came, saying: Lord, thy pound hath gained five pounds. And he said to him: Be thou also over five cities. And another came, saying: Lord, behold here is thy pound, which I have kept laid up in a napkin; for I feared thee, because thou art an austere man: Thou takest up what thou didst not lay down, and thou reapest that which thou didst not sow. He saith to him: Out of thy own mouth I judge thee, thou wicked servant. Thou knewest that I was an austere man, taking up what I laid not down, and reaping that which I did not sow: And why then didst thou not give my money into the bank, that at my coming I might have exacted it with usury? And he said to them that stood by: Take the pound away from him, and give it to him that hath ten pounds. And they said to him: Lord, he hath ten pounds. But I say to you, that to every one that hath shall be given, and he shall abound: and from him that hath not, even that which he hath, shall be taken from him. But as for those my enemies, who would not have me reign over them, bring them hither, and kill them before me" (Lk 19:11–27).*

EXPLANATION: The above parable was spoken by our Lord to His disciples and faithful followers while on His last journey up to Jerusalem. He had come down from Galilee by the Jordan valley working many miracles on the way. At Jericho he had healed the blind man and had visited the house of Zaccheus, "a despised sinful publican," and proclaimed that Zaccheus, too, was a son of Abraham, worthy therefore of the master's attention. This had shocked many faithful followers whose idea of the messianic kingdom was still very Jewish, i.e., that sinners and publicans could have no part in it.

This parable, then, was a corrective both to his followers who wanted Him to reign over them, but according to their ideas, and to His enemies who would not have Him reign over them in any capacity.

A certain nobleman went into a far country, to receive for himself a kingdom: The story He tells to bring out His spiritual lesson was familiar to His hearers. Palestine and the Middle East at the time formed part of the Roman empire. Crowns changed heads almost as frequently as chips change hands in Monte Carlo. An hereditary prince had to go in person to Rome to beg for his kingdom on his father's death, and the same ship often carried three or more

* In Mt 25:14–30 we have the parable of the talents which is so like this parable of the pounds that many authors think they are but one parable given with variations by Luke and Matthew. The truth most likely is that our Lord propounded this parable more than once and that the variations were from Him and not from the Evangelists. He added new details to fit the occasion. As this one of the pounds contains all that the parable of the talents has, we omit the latter for the sake of brevity.

rival claimants as well as delegations from the people requesting that none of these should reign.

A certain nobleman: The claimant in this story is of royal blood; he has a right by birth to the kingdom. How applicable in this case is the word "nobleman," representing Christ as it does!

Went into a far country: This and the directions given his servants indicate clearly that a long time will elapse before the kingdom is finally established. These first words are clearly a check on the overenthusiastic expectations of those who think the Messias' kingdom will be set up in the immediate future.

And calling his ten servants, he gave them pounds, and said to them: Trade till I come: Ten is often used to indicate the total. It stands here for the servants, the followers, in opposition to the enemies mentioned in the following verse. The nobleman distributed some of his possessions among them, and told them to employ these gifts profitably during his absence. The sum, "a pound" (equal to a laborer's wages for a hundred days), seems a paltry sum for a prince to give, but how many of the impoverished princes of the time could give even this much before they received their kingdom? And in the parable the smallness of the sum has a forceful meaning; the followers of Christ, even the Apostles, were still looking for earthly gain for themselves and financial reward for their fidelity to their Master. Here is a second damper on their erroneous enthusiasm: they will receive little or no temporal emoluments. Instead, suffering, hardship, and hard labor will be their lot in His service.

Trade till I come: Not only to survive but to produce profit on such a paltry capital was surely no easy task, and yet this is what the nobleman expected of his followers.

But his citizens hated him: As we said above, every claimant to a throne had his partisans and his opponents; the latter left no stone unturned to prevent his ruling over them. In the parable the opponents of Christ are the Pharisees and leaders of the Jews, who within a few days after this parable was spoken, openly chose Caesar, the hated pagan Roman, as their king, rather than the divinely sent Messias.

And it came to pass, that he returned, having received the kingdom: That there was a long interval is clear from the "far country" to which the prince had journeyed, and from the amount of profit reaped by the diligent traders. The prince has received the kingdom, and he is now in a position to reward his faithful followers and to punish those who rebelled against him.

He commanded his servants to be called: He deals with the faithful first. Each one must render an account of his "trading." The gifts were given for a purpose; the king will now find out if and how each one attained that purpose.

Lord, thy pound hath gained ten pounds. In true humility, this trader gives all the credit to his master's pound, and claims none for himself. A tenfold increase was certainly creditable, and the king does not fail to reward the servant who produced it.

Well done, thou good servant, because thou hast been faithful in a little, thou shalt have power over ten cities: The new king needs governors for the various cities of his kingdom. He now chooses them from those who proved their zeal and fidelity in working for his interests during his absence. Each one will be rewarded in accordance with fidelity he has displayed, but the reward given is beyond all proportion to the temporal fruits produced by the traders.

The second came, saying: Lord, thy pound hath gained five pounds: The profit made by the second trader is only half that of the first, but it is still a proof of great effort, and the trader is rewarded accordingly.

Another came, saying: Lord, behold here is thy pound, which I have kept laid up in a napkin: This third servant has ignored the command he received to trade with the pound given him. He put it safely aside and refused to use it. He was busy working for himself in the meantime, and had no time to work for his future king. The excuse he gives is a false one: "I feared thee because thou art an austere man," for as the king says, if he really feared him he would have worked all the more zealously. There is also more than a hint at injustice on the part of the king: "Thou takest up what thou didst not lay down, and thou reapest that which thou didst not sow." The king is accused of reaping the fruits of others' labors — falsely, as the sequel shows, for the servants are not only allowed to keep what they gained, but also they get a superabundant reward.

The king shows him his excuse is not valid. It was not fear of losing the pound, but unwillingness to work for the king, or rather for the prince whom he probably thought would never become king, that made this servant let the pound lie idle, and it is because of this the king takes the pound from him and gives him no position in his kingdom. He has proved himself disloyal and unworthy.

Lord, he hath ten pounds: The bystanders are astonished at the generosity of the king, who gives the unworthy servant's pound to him who already had the ten his own pound had earned, but the generous king liberally rewards those who are loyal to him. The first servant's profits prove how faithfully and zealously he had worked for his master, and his master will not be outdone in generosity.

From him that hath not, even that which he hath shall be taken from him: In the parable this means that the disloyal servants will not only lose their place in the kingdom of heaven, but also the very gifts of body and soul with which they should have earned heaven will be taken from them.

It will be noted that the nobleman distributed ten pounds among the servants before his departure. But on his return he demands an account of only three. The ten, as we said above, signify all his followers, to each he gave sufficient with which to earn a place in his kingdom on his return. The three who are called to render an account represent the three classes into which his followers can be divided: the very zealous, the zealous, and the negligent.

But as for those my enemies: Having dealt with his followers (real and nominal), he now metes out just punishment to those who openly rebel against him.

Kill them before me: Rebels, according to the custom of the times, were put to death in the very presence of the king. In the parable the rebels are the Pharisees and leaders of the Jews, who almost as a body rejected Christ and would not have Him as their Messias. The destruction of Jerusalem, some forty years later, was the beginning of the terrible reckoning demanded of them by God whom they had rejected. But this event, dreadful as it was, was only a prelude to and a figure of the final destruction which will befall God's enemies at the general judgment.

APPLICATION: When our Lord spoke this parable the week before His crucifixion, it conveyed a lesson both to His followers and to His opponents. To the latter the lesson was that even though they despised and rejected Him, He would reign as king over them, and if they remained obdurately rebellious, they would be excluded from His kingdom and be condemned to everlasting death. For His followers the lesson to be learned was that His kingdom was not a temporal one to be set up in the immediate future, in which there would be peace and plenty, demanding no effort on their part. Instead, His kingdom would have its fulfillment in the distant future, and must be earned through great personal sacrifices and strivings.

Like all of our Lord's words, this parable is as applicable today as it was nineteen centuries ago. The world today in relation to Christ and His eternal kingdom is divided as it was in first-century Palestine. Among His followers there are the truly zealous, the zealous, and the nominal adherents. His opponents today are against Him for the very same reasons as were the Pharisees and leaders of the Jews. They want their messianic kingdom here on earth, a kingdom of pleasure and plenty; they want no limits set on their freedom to sin. Their pride in their own self-exalted dignity will not let them bow the head to any deity which does not conform to their standards. Like the Pharisees, they keep on trying to convince themselves, against the weight of all the evidence, that Christ will not reign, that there will be no day of reckoning. Yet with all their efforts to stifle the small inner voice of conscience which has the nasty habit of reminding them of their folly, they have their troubled moments when the Epicurean motto: "Eat, drink, sleep, and make merry" does not somehow ring true.

For those who are striving to follow Christ, this parable has a message of encouragement and consolation. The road seems hard and strewn with obstacles; the battle against the devil, the world and the flesh seems never-ending. Our means of survival seem paltry and insufficient, yet the Prince who is God knows all our needs, and has given to each one what is meet and just. He has guaranteed us the victory if we do what in us lies. Let us ever keep the day of reckoning before our minds and our present trials will appear in their proper proportions.

For the nominal followers of Christ the parable has a somber warning. It clearly shows that in order to earn heaven it is not enough to be a Christian in name — one must be a Christian in action. Eternal happiness is the divine reward for an earthly service faithfully rendered. The false excuse of the third servant is repeated in many forms among us still: "God is too austere." "He couldn't expect me to make such sacrifices." "I have to provide for myself; maybe His threats and promises are empty words." "He may never return as king to demand a reckoning." These and all other excuses are proved false in this parable.

God is a kind father who has your eternal interest at heart. He does expect you to make the sacrifices. He showed you the way on Calvary. When working for

God you are really providing for yourself; His external glory and your eternal happiness are the fruits of the same labor. He will return to demand a reckoning — it will be too late then to make any changes. Make them now and put your books in order.

THE LABOURERS IN THE VINEYARD

"The kingdom of heaven is like to an householder, who went out early in the morning to hire labourers into his vineyard. And having agreed with the labourers for a penny a day, he sent them into his vineyard. And going out about the third hour, he saw others standing in the market place idle. And he said to them: Go you also into my vineyard, and I will give you what shall be just. And they went their way. And again he went out about the sixth and the ninth hour, and did in like manner. But about the eleventh hour he went out and found others standing, and he saith to them: Why stand you here all the day idle? They say to him: Because no man hath hired us. He saith to them: Go you also into my vineyard. And when evening was come, the lord of the vineyard saith to his steward: Call the labourers and pay them their hire, beginning from the last even to the first. When therefore they were come, that came about the eleventh hour, they received every man a penny. But when the first also came, they thought that they should receive more: and they also received every man a penny. And receiving it they murmured against the master of the house. Saying: These last have worked but one hour, and thou hast made them equal to us, that have borne the burden of the day and the heats. But he answering said to one of them: Friend, I do thee no wrong: didst thou not agree with me for a penny? Take what is thine, and go thy way: I will also give to this last even as to thee. Or, is it not lawful for me to do what I will? is thy eye evil, because I am good? So shall the last be first, and the first last. For many are called, but few chosen" (Mt 20:1–16).

EXPLANATION: Our Lord used this parable to show that man's eternal reward is a free gift of God, a gift infinitely beyond the merits of any human being. It cannot be earned by any work of ours, no matter how strenuous. The Pharisees foolishly held that they had an exclusive right to membership in this kingdom, because they were the Chosen People of the Old Testament, and they strongly objected to Christ's teaching that sinners and publicans could and would have a place in "their" kingdom.

The kingdom of heaven is like to an householder, who went out early in the morning to hire labourers into his vineyard: It was, and still is, the custom in Palestine for those seeking work to come into the towns and villages about daybreak and gather in the square or bazaar to await the coming of the local landowners, who hired the help they needed for the work then on hand. Workers were hired for a month or a week or a day according to the needs of the employer, and the wage was fixed by mutual agreement.

Having agreed with the labourers: The householder in the parable selected a number of men for a day's work, and agreed to pay them the common day's wage of the time, a penny.

Going out about the third . . . sixth and the ninth hour: The Roman method of reckoning the day as twelve hours from 6 a.m. to 6 p.m. was in use in Palestine at the time of our Lord, and so the literal meaning of the first, third, sixth, ninth, and eleventh hours is 6 a.m.; 9 a.m.; 12 noon; 3 p.m.; and 5 p.m. The householder hired men at these different hours of the day, perhaps because the amount of work he wanted done that day was greater than he realized, and this became apparent only as the day wore on. Or more likely, our Lord used this means to emphasize the point He was trying to make.

I will give you what shall be just: The householder offers a just wage, and it is accepted evidently gladly, for as a part of the day had already passed the chances of getting any employment were few.

But about the eleventh hour: He calls another group to his vineyard. He asks them why they stood there idle all day; there is only about one hour of the working day left. They answer, that no one had hired them; this may or may not have been their fault; nevertheless, the householder calls them to work for him and makes no mention of reward. The laborers do not raise the question of reward, because of the late hour, for evidently they left it to his generosity.

Call the labourers: When the day's work is ended, the householder tells the steward to call the laborers together and pay them, beginning with the latest arrivals. This arrangement was necessary for the lesson of the story: had those who worked from early morning been paid first they would most likely have gone away and would not have seen what the others got.

That came about the eleventh hour, they received every man a penny: The householder had made no contract with them, but out of sheer generosity he gives them a full day's wage. He does likewise with those of the ninth, sixth, and third hours. These raise no question, for they too have received more than they expected.

But when the first also came: They were given the full pay, the penny they contracted for, but they murmured at this. Why should those who had worked only one hour get as much as they were given for the whole day? This seemed to them to be unjust, but was it?

Friend, I do thee no wrong: I have paid you a just wage, the amount you freely agreed on. If I give the same wage to others who worked a much shorter day, that is solely my business. May I not be generous with my own money?

Is thy eye evil, because I am good: In other words, your envious minds turn my generosity into injustice. The householder was perfectly just; he kept his part of the contract with the early workers, and if he gave the same pay to those who came later, he had injured no one, but only showed his generosity. So it is with the granting of eternal happiness — some may attain sanctity through long and arduous penances and mortifications; others may become saints in a few short years or hours maybe, because God gives to these latter extraordinary graces. For all those who reach heaven, the reward is far above anything they have earned. As St. Paul puts it, "I reckon that the sufferings of the present time are not worthy to be compared with the glory to come" (Rom 8:18). Having no claim on God's goodness, we have no right to question His generosity. Both St. Paul, who suffered many hardships for over thirty years for the sake of Christ, and the good thief, who was promised paradise the very day on which he turned from sin, have the joys of heaven through God's generosity only. And for both the reward is infinitely beyond anything they could hope to earn. The question of the various degrees of glory in heaven is not discussed in this parable.

So shall the last be first, and the first last: The lesson to be learned from this story is this: nobody has claims against God. Those who, like the Pharisees, thought that they should have priority in the messianic kingdom, even to the exclusion of others, are told that they will be justly treated by God. There is a place for them in that kingdom if they are worthy of it, but they must not restrict the generosity of God. He is free to give an equal or a higher place to others whom the Pharisees judge unworthy. Repentant sinners, returned prodigals are as dear to the heavenly Father as the elder sons were who stayed at home and according to themselves needed no repentance.

Many are called but few chosen: This last phrase most likely does not belong here, but is an interpolation from Mt 22:14, where its meaning is quite clear.

APPLICATION: The call to the vineyard, through God's gift of faith and the sacrament of baptism, is a gift for which I can never thank God sufficiently. If I remain in the vineyard, and labor honestly, that is, if I co-operate with the actual grace God is continually giving me, I am assured of meriting an increase in sanctifying grace and eventually heaven. Now, the work I have to do in the vineyard is the fulfilling of the duties of my state in life. By carrying out these duties honestly and sincerely, I am doing the will of God and I am saving my soul. The greater part of my day, and indeed of my life, will be taken up with tasks in themselves worldly, but these tasks when done in the state of grace and with the intention of pleasing God have supernatural value. For this we have only the goodness and generosity of God to thank. By calling us to the faith, He has raised us to a supernatural state. Baptism gives us a new birth: "Amen, amen I say to thee, unless a man be born again of water and the Holy Ghost, he cannot enter into the kingdom of God" (Jn 3:5).

He could have made the attainment of heaven so much more difficult. He could have demanded extraordinary mortifications and extreme renunciations, and the reward would still be exceedingly great. Instead, He allows me to live my everyday life, to enjoy the love and friendship of my family and friends, to satisfy the natural desires of the body, within the law, and to merit a supernatural reward while so doing, provided I am in the state of grace and have the right intention. As He tells us through St. Paul: "Whether you eat or drink, or whatever else you do, do all to the glory of God" (1 Cor 10:31).

Looking back on my past life, how many years have I really given to God since I came to the use of reason — those school years, the time spent learning a trade or profession, the weeks, months, years, working in the factory, in the store, in the office, the hours among the pots and pans in the kitchen and pantry? Have I earned some credit in heaven for all this, or is it all crossed off my pay sheet for lack of right intentions, or because I was not in the state of grace? If so, those years are lost to me; I was "idle" all that time. Today's parable, however, should give me new courage. It may be the sixth, or the ninth, or even the eleventh hour of my life, yet I can still earn heaven if I listen to the call today and resolve to work faithfully and diligently in the Lord's vineyard during whatever span of life still remains to me.

And though I am not like the Pharisees, and do not envy God's liberality toward others, is that enough? Does God expect no more of me? Are there not many of God's children, my brothers, standing all day "in the market place idle" waiting for me to bring them God's call? And opportunities to do just this are never wanting. If I truly love God and my neighbor, and if I really appreciate what God's gift of eternal happiness means, I will help a brother to return to the Lord's vineyard where the heavenly penny is waiting for him, no matter how late in the day he might accept the call.

UNPROFITABLE SERVANTS

"But which of you having a servant ploughing, or feeding cattle, will say to him, when he is come from the field: Immediately go, sit down to meat: and will not rather say to him: Make ready my supper, and gird thyself, and serve me, whilst I eat and drink, and afterwards thou shalt eat and drink? Doth he thank that servant, for doing the things which he commanded him? I think not. So you also, when you shall have done all these things that are commanded you say: We are unprofitable servants; we have done that which we ought to do" (Lk 17:7–10).

EXPLANATION: When the seventy-two disciples returned from the mission to the towns and villages of Galilee, they rejoiced because of the great powers Christ had given them. "Even the devils are subject to us in thy name," they said. Our Lord immediately checked this inclination to glory in what was not theirs: "Do not rejoice in this, that the spirits are subject to you" (Lk 10:20). It was very human that the disciples, as yet but beginners in the faith, should be tempted to glory in the marvelous powers given them. But they must learn to overcome this temptation. The present parable serves as a reminder that they must practice true humility. The Apostles had asked for an increase in their faith (cf. 17:5) — that is, an increase of confidence in God. They must not claim for themselves credit for works which belonged to God.

Which of you: This is a way of introducing the illustration or parable. It does not imply that the Apostles or disciples had such servants, but they were familiar with what was expected of servants.

Ploughing, or feeding cattle: This servant's principal occupation was in his master's fields.

When he is come from the field: For a normal servant or farm laborer, this would be the end of his day's work, but this servant was a slave, not a present-day laborer. A slave in those days had no rights, and he was at the beck and call of his master every moment of every day.

Immediately go, sit down to meat: How welcome such an invitation would be to the tired laborer, but it was not to be expected by a slave.

Make ready my supper: The work in the fields gives place to housework. He must now set about preparing his master's evening meal — no easy task, as the evening meal was the principal meal of the day, and then he must wait on his master at table.

Whilst I eat and drink: All this, the preparation of the meal and the waiting at the table, would occupy well over an hour, so the repast was no quick snack.

Afterwards thou shalt eat and drink: The poor slave would get his well-earned meal when his master no longer needed him.

Doth he thank the servant . . . ? This was the ordinary daily routine of a slave in those days, and no master was expected to be grateful to a slave for doing what he was commanded.

So you also: Our Lord now tells the disciples to apply the lesson to themselves. There is no question here of our Lord approving of the inhumanity of slavery, or of the hardheartedness of slave masters — He simply draws a spiritual lesson from the routine life of a slave (just as in other parables He describes a prodigal, a merciless servant, an unjust judge).

When you shall have done all these things that are commanded you: Here He tells His disciples to imitate the slave who expected no reward, and certainly did not demand any from his master. When they have carried out all God demands of them, and this includes even the performing of miracles, they too should say:

We are unprofitable servants: What have we done to add to God's stature? In what way have we benefited Him? What gift of our own did we confer on Him? Rather, all we did was make use of the gifts He gave us. The honor and the glory for anything we, His instruments, did goes to God. The power and the faculties we used were all His.

We have done that which we ought to do: We simply did what was expected of us — we used His gifts as He commanded. That God will reward His faithful servants, even though no one can claim a reward from God in strict justice, is made sufficiently clear in several statements of Christ (see for instance the parables of the laborers in the vineyard, p. 114; the vigilant servants, p. 49; the Pounds, p. 109. But the true disciple must realize like St. Paul that "of himself he can do nothing," but he can "do all things in him who strengthens him." He must, in other words, have a truly humble view of himself in relation to God.

APPLICATION: This parable with its practical lesson was given in the first instance to the Apostles and disciples. Because of the many supernatural powers given them by God for the spread of the infant Church, they might attribute to themselves what belonged to God. But they took their Master's words to heart. They recognized their own nothingness, and consequently were exalted in heaven. But the parable has a lesson for us too. Every gift of body and soul that we have has been given us by God. The master in the parable thought he owned his slave, body and soul, and therefore he expected the slave to devote every moment of his time and every power he possessed to his service. This was the opinion and the law at the time; it was very wrong, but thus it was. God, on the other hand, created us. He is our absolute Master, for He gave us everything we are and have. Have we always admitted this, or have we falsely taken the credit for these gifts as if they were our own? Have we perhaps looked down on a neighbor who did not have as many gifts from God as we have? Have we begrudged being asked to use some of God's gifts for His purposes? Have we sought out the praise of men, or of God, if we did so use them?

There are men and women in the world who shamelessly claim their heavenly gifts as their own; they never acknowledge God as their benefactor. There are Christians, and Catholics too, who are ready to grumble at any little demand God makes on their time, their health, or their money. Should they not instead thank God that they are able to return a small portion of His gift; should they not be grateful for having the loan of these gifts for so long free of interest? Others spend their bodily and spiritual gifts generously in God's service, but they expect the praise of God and of men for it, and thus ruin their gifts. Such sinful pride turned the good works of the Pharisees into means of self-glorification, not God's glorification. Our Lord warned us about this vice when He said: "Take heed that you do not your justice before men, to be seen by them . . . when thou dost an almsdeed, sound not a trumpet before thee, as the hypocrites do . . . that they may be honoured by men. . . . And when you pray, you shall not be as the hypocrites, that love to stand and pray in the synagogues and corners of the streets, that they may be seen by men" (Mt 6:1–8). And it is this same lesson and warning He is giving us in the present parable. If we used every gift of body and soul that we have, and if we gladly surrendered our lives in martyrdom for God, what have we done but returned His own gifts to Him? That God allows us to work for Him is a privilege, not a favor He needs from us. The great Apostles and missionaries of the Church converted countless souls in their lifetime — St. Paul, St. Patrick, St. Boniface, St. Francis, St. Dominic, St. Solanus, St. Xavier — yet God, unaided, could have converted these souls in an instant. To use a homely illustration, in helping God we are like the little girl of four who "helps" her mother in the kitchen; she is perhaps more a hindrance than a help, but the good mother allows her to do the little bit she can so that she may prove to her mother that she loves her. All the great saints grasped this lesson fully. They realized that their greatest efforts were as little grains of sand on the seashore when offered to the infinite God. Their only cause of grief was not how much they were called to do, but the littleness, the insignificance of all they could do.

And if the saints of God felt that their sacrifices on earth were paltry and insignificant, how should we feel about our puny efforts? Look back today on your past life: of the twenty, forty, sixty years God has given you on earth, how many hours a week have you really given to God? Of the many gifts and talents of body and soul He lent you, how often did you use any or all of them in His service? Of the worldly goods, which God in His goodness have given to you or to your parents, how much of them have you shared with your neighbor who was not so blessed by God?

Our Lord does not say our good works are useless or not acceptable to God, but we must not see in them something of our very own which gives us a strict claim on God, but rather the returning to God of some of His many favors to us. That God's infinite goodness and generosity deign to reward us eternally for our puny efforts is entirely because of our kind heavenly Father. While thanking Him sincerely for this merciful kindness, let us resolve to go on offering in all humility our tiny helping hand wherever and whenever we can until He tells us, like the slave in the parable, to sit down to eat at the heavenly Banquet.